Effectiveness:

"Producing

a decided,

decisive, or

desired effect."

MERRIAM-WEBSTER'S
2019 UNABRIDGED DICTIONARY

MISSION: POSSIBLE

A Simple Structure
for Missional Effectiveness

Revised and Expanded Second Edition

by Kay Kotan and Blake Bradford

Foreword by John Edmund Kaiser

Epilogue by Bishop Robert Farr

Market
Square

MISSION POSSIBLE

A Simple Structure for Missional Effectiveness

Revised and Expanded Second Edition

©2019 Kay Kotan and Blake Bradford

books@marketsquarebooks.com
P.O. Box 23664 Knoxville, Tennessee 37933

ISBN: 978-1-7323092-7-2
Library of Congress: 2019936252
Printed and Bound in the United States of America
Cover Illustration & Book Design ©2019 Market Square Publishing, LLC
Publisher: Kevin Slimp
Editor: Kristin Lighter
Post-Process Editor: Ken Rochelle

Table of Contents

Foreword

If your United Methodist congregation is able to have Kay Kotan serve as its consultant and coach, two things are true: you will have an easier path to cleaning up your leadership structure, and this book of hers will give you a head start on that path. If you are not able to have Kay Kotan in person, this book, *Mission Possible*, is the next best thing. Either way, you have your hands on the right tool.

Women and men who have been involved in church leadership for any length of time are well acquainted with the fallout from ineffective organizational structure. Nothing gets done. Time gets wasted. Purpose gets lost. People get hurt.

Leadership structure in your congregation is a little like bone structure in your body. It isn't what life is all about. Normally you hardly even see it. But when it is broken or twisted, the pain and dysfunction can drive you crazy. Fortunately, like broken bones, broken leadership structure can be reset.

About ten years ago, Abingdon Press published my first book, *Winning on Purpose: Organizing Congregations to Succeed in Their Mission.* It grew out of the training mate-

1

rial I had developed on what I called "Accountable Leadership." As with any useful resource, it owed a lot to those who had influenced my work. Chief among those influencers were Paul Borden, John Carver, and Leith Anderson. With the publication of *Mission Possible*, I am gratified to see my work augmented and applied through Kay Kotan.

While *Winning on Purpose* was designed to be useful for as wide a range of Christian movements as possible, *Mission Possible* is focused like a laser on the practical needs and challenges of United Methodist congregations. Here are some of the things I particularly like about the book.

The style of writing is personal, encouraging, and to the point. Your time will not be wasted, and you will get the sense that a savvy consultant is at your elbow to guide you along the process of simplifying the structure of your congregation. You'll find good counsel here. There is a wisdom that comes only from working through the issues with multiple ministry contexts over a period of years, and the author clearly has paid her dues. She knows what she is talking about.

The opportunities and obstacles inherent in UMC polity and policy inform the step-by-step process for change that is recommended. What to work through and what to work around has all been taken into consideration.

The checklists in each chapter leave no doubt as to the order in which to proceed and the factors that must be accounted for. There is appropriate attention to detail. When you feel like asking, "But then what do we do?" all that is needed is to turn the page. The FAQ section is especially helpful.

These days whenever you purchase a new piece of

technology, the included user's manual typically comes in multiple languages. In short, Kay Kotan has written an excellent user's manual in the language of the UMC for the kind of simple and effective leadership strategy that we both believe in. Why do we believe in it? Because it works.

So, if you care about the fruitfulness of your congregation's time, money, and effort, keep this little book close at hand. Some assembly required.

John Kaiser

Acknowledgements

This book is dedicated to the hundreds of churches and pastors who have invited us into their ministry. Thank you for the opportunity to journey with you and serve alongside you. It is because of you that we have had the experiences to share with others so that they might benefit from your challenges and achievements.

Introduction

I (Kay) have had the privilege of taking a few cruises in the past twenty years. They are always enjoyable. It is a great time of relaxation, sunny weather, and beautiful destinations. There are no worries. Someone else does the grocery shopping, plans the meals, prepares the meals, does dishes, makes my bed, mops the floor, cleans my room, pilots the boat, manages all the port clearances, shuffles my luggage to my room, entertains me, etc. It is truly a vacation from reality. It is an escape! It seems so easy and carefree from a passenger standpoint, but there are hundreds of employees behind the scenes orchestrating this experience. There is a captain leading this cohesive team with a single focus working collaboratively to create this dream experience for all its passengers.

Now can you image that same cruise ship out in the Caribbean allowing only the weather, wind, and tides to determine its destination? We would never dream of allowing such a thing to occur. There is no way anyone would allow a multi-million-dollar boat with thousands of people to toss aimlessly in the waves without a predetermined destination. Some passengers may have embarked the ship with a desire to go to Aruba while others had a desired destination of Alaska. Without a map, pathway, itinerary, or captain directing the way and the people, the experience would be quite different. Yet, this is how many of our churches today operate. No one is directing the ship with a commonly understood destination and course. We are simply being tossed about by the sea of life and frustrated that we are not getting anywhere. No one has their eye on the mission – making disciples!

Mission NOT Accomplished/Possible

W. Edwards Deming, a postwar engineer and scientist of manufacturing systems, proclaimed that "every system is perfectly designed to get the result that it does." The mainline churches' congregational governance structure is designed with multiple layers of checks and balances. Our inherited governance and leadership structure is a system built to maintain and preserve the ecclesiastical institution, to make sure that nothing too crazy (or creative) happens. While this may have been fine in the American postwar era of church growth and engagement, the missional church of the twenty-first century must be creative and structurally enabled to make nimble changes in methods to fulfill its disciple-making tradition.

The typical church structure is driving the mission rather than the mission driving the structure! We are simply not accomplishing the mission Jesus intended for our churches. Due to the way in which we are structured, the mission is sometimes not even possible! To make matters worse, most of us know this, yet many of us are not willing or able to change it. Our churches get mired down in the "way we have always done things" and find it difficult, if not impossible, to change the "way we have always done things."

All the churches we work with desire to reach new people (of course, mostly young people with children). Yet, some are not willing to make the changes to make this happen. We cannot count the times churches "say" they want to reach people, but when it comes down to making the changes to actually reach new people, many dig their heels in and resist the change. Mostly this is because the changes will affect those people personally. If changes only affect others, the changes are acceptable. However, once they become personal, changes are much more difficult to accept.

Do you believe the mission is possible? Do you want the mission to succeed? Do you *really* want the mission to succeed? If the answer is yes, we must align all that we do as churches and individual disciples to the mission of making disciples of Jesus Christ for the transformation of the world. Yes, making disciples is the very reason each and every church exists. Jesus designed the church to continue His work in spreading the Good News. So again, do we want to the mission to succeed? Really? We have always loved this quote from Tom Bandy about putting the very important missional question into perspective:

> *"Are you prepared to stake everything, change **anything**, and do **whatever** it takes – even if it means altering long familiar habits, redeveloping precious programs, and redeploying sacred assets?"*
> **Tom Bandy, From the foreword of Winning On Purpose**

There is hope! There is another way forward. There are options where faithfulness for reaching the mission is more possible than others. We must structure our churches today to be lean, effective, and efficient if we are to impact our non-church centric world. We can simply no longer function in our archaic structures and methods if we are to reach the people of today for Jesus Christ. The structure in many of our churches is holding us back from accomplishing our mission. In some churches the current structure and methods do not allow us to keep our eye on the ball. We are so busy running our structure, that the structure is running us! Our mission is no longer our focus. And without focus, the mission will not succeed.

Our motivation for providing this resource is multi-fold. Kay has been working as a coach, consultant, and conference staff with churches and pastors across the country trying to make structural changes for over a decade now. In addition to pastoral service in large and small churches, Blake has served on conference staff and as district superintendent, which has afforded him the opportunity to see leaders and structures from a wide cross-section of contexts. The same pitfalls are observed repeatedly. Our hope and prayer in providing this resource is to first help churches really understand what they are undertaking before deciding to move forward. Secondly, we hope this resource will help churches navigate the process with eyes wide open and the tools needed to do so. Finally, we hope this resource provides the outcome of fruitful and effective ministries to reach new people for Jesus Christ.

This book will lead you through both the technical and adaptive shifts that will need to be addressed to align your church to the mission of making disciples. If you came to this book looking for only the technical "how-to's" for moving into simplified structure so you can have fewer meetings, you may be a bit frustrated. Our intention is to challenge you to move beyond making this just a technical change, but to also move you through this very large adaptive change. It is in the adaptive change that churches

8

can create a whole new trajectory of vitality with a deeper impact.

If you are ready to partake in a bold, brave journey for you and your church towards faithfulness in fruitful ministries, let the journey begin!

A Few Disclaimers

Terminology: Simplified vs Single Board

You might have heard what we are referring to as "simplified structure" as the "single board model." Indeed, when I (Kay) first began to work with simplifying church structure, we referred to this practice as the single board model with accountable leadership. I try to no longer use the terminology of the single board. Here is my reasoning. When churches heard "single board," some interpreted that to mean that there were no other committees or teams except for the one leadership team. These churches no longer had ministries teams or even a Nominations Committee. The church simply stopped ministry and only had worship. This was a huge misunderstanding and was difficult to course-correct. In fact, there was one particular church that almost closed due to this misunderstanding! No one wants that to happen, so we changed the terminology we now use to describe changing structure. We now refer to this shift as simplified, accountable leadership.

Personal Interpretation

Provided herein is our own personal interpretation and application of the United Methodist Church's *Book of Discipline (BOD)* as it pertains to structuring a local church through our coaching and consulting in hundreds of churches. Refer to your District Superintendent, Cabinet, Bishop and Annual Conference for confirmation as local interpretations that might differ. Understand that your conference or district may also have additional policies that require modifying our advice or Disciplinary interpretations.

United Methodist Centered

Many times, the *BOD* is referenced in these writings and our experience is mostly from United Methodist Churches. If you are not United Methodist, please make sure you apply your own church polity to these writings.

Keep it Simple for Christ's Sake:
Two Ecclesiastical Parables

It almost seemed like the system was designed to make sure ministry would not happen. A member had an idea: "What if we converted our annual Easter Egg Hunt, a nice little gathering of our church membership's families, into an opportunity to meet more of the neighborhood, bless the families of the community, and perhaps get contact information that might be followed-up on as an act of evangelism?" A ministry team was formed. The idea continued to hatch, and a cookout and kids' fair was dreamed up and planned by the team. A member who was a grocer pledged to donate the food. The leader of the children's ministry and the pastor were fully on board, and so was the Church Council, but a change to our normal way of doing things required some permissions, to make sure no one would get upset. The Church Council wanted to make sure that the other committees of the church would not get upset by a usurpation of their power. First, the Trustees would need to get involved, since the idea included using the Church's front lawn at the center of town. Then the team would need approval of the finance committee, to approve shifting of the budgeted children's ministry funds from one line item to another. After those two committees met and each approved the plan, the Council would make its final determination. It is too bad that the series of scheduled meetings would require that the idea for an Easter event would receive its final approval in June!

Meetings are not ministry. The system of committee-based checks and balances that was suited for the days of mid-twentieth century Christendom is no longer an effective way to mobilize the people-power and resources of the Church in our twenty-first century interconnected world in which the church no longer is at the center of community life. We need a nimble structure that can respond to fresh ideas and approaches to ministry. We United Methodists can, at times, get distracted by our desire for consensus and lose sight of our actual mission. Leaders (lay and clergy alike) need to be allowed and empowered to lead. Meetings need to actually matter and operate as moments for accountability and missional alignment.

A simplified accountable governing structure makes it possible for your church to better focus on leadership equipping, missional alignment, and your next steps in ministry. Meanwhile, removing bureaucratic redundancies allows more members to spend their time in service as disciples who make disciples. By consolidating administrative functions into a single board, disciples can focus on using their spiritual gifts and passions for ministry to contribute to the vitality of the congregation as it seeks to reach the mission field.

So, let's imagine another story. A member is blessed with a great idea to connect to the community during the Easter season. A ministry team engages with the idea and improves upon it, getting volunteers lined up and a donation from a member. Staff rearrange their budgets under the existing authority they have been given. Because the change involves a huge cultural shift in the way the church has historically experienced the Easter season, the pastor asks the simplified structure Leadership Board to consider the change.

Since the change fits into the mission, vision, and evangelistic goals of the congregation, the Council celebrates the new idea and commends the ministry team leading the effort. Eight weeks later, at the new Community Egg Hunt and Cookout, dozens of guests experience the relational hospitality of the congregation, and contact information is collected at an Easter Bunny Photo Booth for follow-up. New friendships are created and new disciples begin their discipleship journey through the ministry of the church.

Structured to Thrive

It is for the sake of Christ and His mission that our congregations exist. By simplifying our church structures, we are creating an environment where ministry can thrive. Vital and fruitful churches must be governed and led in new ways today so that Christ's mission for us can be fulfilled! The disciple-making mission which Christ has given us is too important to let bureaucratic redundancies distract us from our work. For the sake of Christ's mission and our mission fields, many churches are discovering that there are simpler ways to provide governance and strategic direction so that the congregation can be unleashed for ministry.

CHAPTER ONE
Discerning the Shift

Fewer people making decisions is NOT the goal of moving to a simplified, accountable leadership structure. The goal of any change in structure must ultimately be about successfully implementing the mission/purpose of the organization. For churches, that mission is making disciples of Jesus Christ to transform the world. You need a governing and strategic structure that will help make this holy mission a reality. Some seek this change in governance because the number of active members does not allow for filling all the disciplinary committees as separate entities. While a simplified structure may help to solve that dilemma, it should never be the ultimate purpose. Simplifying your structure is not about consolidating power, it is about making the congregation's decision-making nimbler and unleashing lay leadership for more ministry!

Often when we teach church leaders about simplified, accountable leadership structure, someone in the crowd will share a metaphor about moving deck chairs on the Titanic. There is a truth under the statement. It is certainly correct that a change in structure will not fix relational difficulties or missional apathy. Simplified, accountable leadership structure could, however, create clarity in roles, connect responsibility and authority, and bring missional focus to your congregation and its leadership. To return to the metaphor about deck chairs on the sinking ship, simplified, accountable leadership structure isn't about the deck chairs, it is about the leadership. It is Titanic's captain, its officers, and its owners that ignored the radio warnings about icebergs, that failed to provide lookout officers with binoculars and searchlights, that turned the ship the wrong way, that decided to travel full-speed through icy waters, and that under-equipped the ship with lifeboats. The deck chairs were fine. It was the folks on the ship's bridge that caused the trouble. Simplified, accountable leadership structure is about who is on the "ship's bridge" and how they are empowered (and held accountable) to lead the church in fulfilling its disciple-making mission.

We also offer a warning that we shared in our book *Impact! Reclaiming the Call of Lay Ministry*, "Changing the number of people around the leadership table without also changing the leadership culture will only result in an isolated and ineffective board." The twenty-first chapter of the Gospel of John is instructive here. After the resurrected Jesus had appeared to Mary, the gathered disciples, and to Thomas in John Chapter 20, Peter went back to what he knew best -- fishing in Lake Galilee. He even went back to fishing on the same comfortable side of the boat, and they were catching nothing. It took another appearance of Jesus for them to try fishing from the other side of the boat, and this time their net was filled to capacity! It was so filled that they couldn't even haul their net into the boat! After a meal with the Risen Christ, Peter and Jesus had some words, including Jesus' imperative, "Follow Me!" Peter couldn't go back to comfortable habits and remain fruitful in Christ. He had to *change* to become the disciple Jesus needed him to be to fulfill God's mission.

That is why your ***why*** is so important. We have both seen many churches that changed their structure, but they did not change their behaviors. They continued to use the same agenda and the same decision-making processes, and they kept on having the same conversations at the table. After becoming frustrated, they either reached out for help or scrapped the whole process. A clear ***why*** moves a structural change from just being a technical modification into being a transformative opportunity.

Who Are We Now?

In order to get to your deep ***why*** of a new structure, you and your fellow church leaders need to fully understand and be able to describe the structure of your current leadership system. How does your church make decisions and set goals now? Does your official nominations report submitted and approved at Charge Conference actually reflect your system of governance, or are there unwritten rules or unelected people, such as a matriarch or patriarch, that has a de facto veto power over all your church's decisions? Also, be honest with yourselves as a church. If your congregation has lingering issues of mistrust or a history of power-grabbing cliques, then a change in governance structure will not be a magic wand. Instead, it will probably deepen and intensify your internal mistrust. Congregational health and a re-focus on Christ's mission for the church must come first.

As you consider your current leadership structure, think in terms of it as a system. Often when we work with congregations to articulate a description of their current structure, especially in smaller churches, we are told about the people and their relationships to each other. While relationships are vitally important in ministry, now is the time to think systematically -- roles, responsibilities, limits to authority, policies, and committee job descriptions.

In preparation for discussions of a structure change, perform a leadership inventory and audit:

1. What is the total number of elected leadership positions in your church, compared to total active membership? What is the percentage of active members who are in elected leadership? (We have seen churches where 90 percent or more of the congregation is in elected leadership, which might be understand-able in very small congregations, but it is a recipe for leadership inertia in mid-size churches -- if everyone is in charge, then no one is in charge.)

2. How many leaders are currently in administrative/ governance leadership (finance, trustees, SPRC, administrative board) versus the number of members in programmatic/ministry leadership (worship, evan-gelism, etc.)?

3. How many leaders sit on more than one committee?

4. Think through the past few years and consider two or three large projects that your leadership had to approve. In those cases, how many committees were required to be involved to make a decision? How long did the entire approval process take, from conception to implementation to writing the thank-you notes?

5. How does your existing structure, both in reality and in written Charge Conference submissions, conform to the requirements of the *United Methodist Book of*

Discipline (or other denominational book of policy standards for our non-UMC readers).

Your answers to these questions will give you the contextual background information you will need as you consider a new way of leading your congregation. Now you are ready to begin considering why a new structure might enable your congregation to be more intentional in your discipleship processes, to focus more on creative opportunities beyond your walls, and to more effectively manage the fiduciary responsibilities of the congregation.

The Why

Before making any change, whether it be in governance or in implementing a new ministry, we must first begin with the *why*. So many times, when organizations go through changes, we lead with the "what" and the "how." We communicate what we desire or what steps we need to accomplish. However, it is most helpful to lead with the *why*. In other words, *why* is this change needed? *Why* will this change make a difference in the life of the congregation? People are often more motivated by the *why* than the "what." In our experience, when we lead with the "what," people come to their own conclusions about the *why*. These self-conclusions are often misled because they were not well-informed.

To help in determining the *why*, you might even think about using a SWOT analysis for communicating the need for change. A SWOT analysis is a strategic planning technique that includes a study of the internal strengths and weaknesses of the organization, mapped out in comparison to the external opportunities and threats the organization faces. Begin with describing all that is going well

in the church (strengths) and consider how your current
structure is using your resources, including leaders, their
spiritual gifts, and their time. Next, describe the motivating factors that created the conversation about a possible
change. Describe the obstacles and challenges that keeping
your current structure will create or sustain, along with an
honest evaluation of the costs of making a structural change
(weaknesses). Then, it is time to look beyond your walls
and stained-glass windows to external factors. Start by
imagining the way a new structure will enable the congregation to make faster and more holistic decisions on behalf
of the church to make disciples and impact the world (opportunities). Finally, explain what would be the possible outcome
for the church's mission if the change is not made (threats).

SWOT Analysis for a Structure Change

	Strengths	Weaknesses	Opportunities	Threats
Assess Your Current Leadership Structure	What is working well? What is the best part of how you are currently using resources and people?	What isn't working so well? What are your motives for keeping the current structure? Are the motives missional or for other reasons, such as protecting "turf" or entitlement?	How does your structure respond to new ministry ideas or creative solutions? How proactive is your current board in actually looking for opportunities, taking risks, and setting the strategic direction of the congregation?	How will your congregation make disciples of Jesus Christ to transform the world in our complex, fast changing culture that is very different than the one in which our structure was built?
Imagine a New Simplified Accountable Leadership Structure	How might a change be a better use of resources and people?	What are the costs of shifting to a new simplified, accountable leadership structure, particularly in the area of relationships and trust? How might you mitigate the negative effects of the change, especially among those who feel a loss of power?	What opportunities are you missing, either because of lack of alignment or the overworking of the same people for multiple committees? Imagine how the well-aligned and nimble board might be able to claim opportunities.	How do you imagine the simplified, accountable leadership board will be able to engage our complex and fast-moving world differently to lead the church in fulfilling our mission?

Motivating Factors

Most churches we work with find one or more of the following four elements to be the driving motivators in considering structure changes: efficiency, alignment, missional focus, and accountability.

Efficiency. In its traditional structure, many church decisions must run through multiple committees. Not only are there multiple stops on the permission train, but the train schedule is not efficient! One must sometimes wait a month or more for the next scheduled meeting on the permission train schedule. Those trying to work the process often find themselves discouraged, frustrated, and may even give up! Churches also many times have all their congregation tied up in administrative tasks leaving no one to do the ministry! I (Kay) once worked with a church with about a hundred in worship attendance and had nearly one hundred thirty committee seats to fill. In the Arkansas Conference, one of our key points of Bishop Gary Mueller's Mission Plan is to "Unleash Lay Leadership." The more time that disciples are dealing with administrative issues, the less time they have for ministry in the neighborhood. By simplifying governing structures, more leaders can then unleash spiritual gifts of leadership to work toward ministry, not meetings.

Alignment. Most churches find themselves working in silos. One team or committee has no idea what the other is doing. Sometimes scheduling or resource conflicts arise. There is internal competition for people power, funding, and staff time. Groups do not seem to all be pulling in the same direction for a common purpose or focus. Some churches often operate as multiple mini-churches or groups within one church. Alignment with the mission and vision is about being faithful to our purpose, not about reaching a consensus. Alignment to our mission and vision needs to be a non-negotiable.

Missional focus. It still astonishes us that if you were to ask the average person in the pew why the church exists, they would most likely give you an answer something like, "to serve me," "to help me grow in my faith," or "to provide pastoral care to the flock." Somewhere along the line we have lost our purpose. We have become a nation of churches where so many have an internal focus of being served rather than an external focus of making disciples.

Accountability. For some reason, there is a belief that because the church is made up mostly of volunteers, no one can be held accountable. Think about that for a minute. If this life is preparing us for eternal life, where did we ever come up with the idea that accountability for fruitfulness in the life of the church is not reasonable? Should this not be the place where we are held *most* accountable? We are Wesleyans, and Methodist Christians have accountability hard-wired into us from our history of class meetings and the early societies and conferences. We need to reclaim this missional accountability today.

Please, please heed this **warning**. If you are considering simplifying your structure, but are unable or unwilling to also begin practicing accountability, don't move into simplification. All churches could practice accountable leadership. Some churches could shift to simplified, accountable leadership. No church should move to simplified, leadership structure without accountability. Time and time again, churches who have moved into simplified structure without accountable leadership have had severe push-back problems, conflict, decline, and flat-out ugliness. It is all but impossible to hold a committee accountable. Individuals are held accountable. Accountability keeps us from falling into the traps of being pastor-centered churches, churches of silos, or churches of controlling cliques. Also, be honest with yourself about your motivations. If the motivation for seeking this change in structure is a pretext or passive-aggressive attempt to get a particular difficult member off a committee, hit the brakes. In those cases, the congregation needs to work on communication, healthy boundaries, and accountability. No structure, no matter how simple or elegant, can fix problems of relational health. We will share more about accountable leadership in Chapter 3.

Once the *why* has been identified and communicated, the church needs to consider the process to move to a new structure with accountable leadership. This is a process that should not be rushed. Sometimes leaders are anxious to "get going" and rush through the execution. This is a fundamental mistake! You are better off to slow the process down and bring people along the best you can than to rush the process. Clear, complete, and patient preparation will pay generous dividends as you move into the process. This intentional process of transition will be the focus of our next chapter.

In each chapter, a checklist will be provided to make sure you capture each step along the way. Following is a checklist for you, your pastor, and your current lay leaders to discern the shift into simplified structure.

Checklist for Discernment

- Read this entire resource before making a decision.
- Complete your SWOT analysis of your current governance compared with a change to simplified, accountable leader-

ship structure. Consider how you might you mitigate the risks and costs involved in a change while still remaining focused on your congregation's mission.

- Know your *why*: Build a clear case for a change using each of the four driving motivators:

  o Efficiency – Our churches must be structured so that leaders can lead, not simply maintain the status quo. Moving toward a permission-giving culture with less meetings and more leaders involved in direct ministry!

  o Alignment of people, funding, facilities, program, and other resources.

  o Missional focus – Moving from self-focus and institutional survival toward incarnational ministry in the lives, neighborhoods, communities, and the larger world.

  o Accountability – When "everyone" is in charge, no one is actually held responsible. Our structure should enable leaders to hold themselves and others account-able for missional fruitfulness.

CHAPTER TWO
Making the Change

You figured out your *why* -- your purpose in making a structural change. Amen! Hopefully your *why* goes well beyond simply having fewer meetings and instead is about leading your congregation to impact your mission field. Now you and your fellow leaders will need to enter a period of continued discernment and intentional communication.

I (Kay) have a confession to make. When I first started working with pastors and churches, simplifying the church structure (how decisions are made) seemed to be a no-brainer. After all, I had lived this model in corporate America and in my own business. Why would not each and every church be running to move to this structure? I had also lived through the pains and struggles of navigating a cumbersome structure in my own church as a layperson. Again, I could not for the life of me understand why churches were not sprinting to their district superintendents' offices to gain permission to move into this. And then it happened ... reality check! What I have come to understand is that this is a very difficult shift for most churches. It is difficult for a host of reasons. Through my coaching and consulting, I have discovered those reasons include lack of trust, fear of change, misunderstanding of the model, misunderstanding of the purpose, lack of transparency, lack of leadership adaptability, unwillingness for leaders to give up their seat, fear of the unknown, and the perception of the power of the church being in too few of hands. Because of all these potential or existing barriers, a church must spend time discerning, preparing, teaching, and communicating about this possible shift *first*.

As a district superintendent, I (Blake) have a few additional reasons to ask that leaders take the transition process patiently and intentionally. As readers of this book and (I'm sure) a researcher of different models of church structuring, you and your team have spent hours poring through the *BOD* and downloading charts and lists. You have discerned your *why*, and you understand the governance architecture of the structure you are building.

Your average church member has not done this homework. While they may trust you enough to vote their approval of a new structure, a problem shows up a year or two later, after the first set of leaders rotate off the board, or when your pastor is appointed to a new congregation. Then the church is left with a governance system that nobody knows how to run. I have spoken with congregational leaders who have then inherited a "sports car of a structure," but nobody in leadership knows how to drive stick.

So, be intentional and patient in communicating the shift to a simplified, accountable leadership structure. We offer ten steps to make the transition, and suggest that you plan the process by projecting dates for each step. You will first notice the checklist with a brief description. Following the checklist, you will find a more comprehensive explanation of each step.

Ten Steps to Transition to Simplified, Accountable Leadership Structure

DATE   **STEP**

_____ 1. Determine why a structure change is needed or desired. Equip your leaders in basic principles of discernment and accountable leadership. Create a draft time-line and plan for discernment, communication of the proposed change, congregational votes, and launch.

_____ 2. Consult your District Superintendent for a preliminary conversation about a potential structure change.

_____ 3. Ensure the congregation is prepared for an accountable leadership model of governance. Prepare for and lead congregational conversations about potential changes utilizing two-way communication. Lead with the *why* and then follow with the "what" and "how".

_____ 4. Uncover and discuss feedback from congregation and use the feedback to build your model for a new leadership structure.

_____ 5. Create a temporary task force, approved by the existing administrative board or church council, to create a draft set of founding guiding principles, and to begin preparing updates for all existing congregational policies (personnel, facility, finance, endowment, by-laws, etc.) so that the policies will be in compliance with proposed structure.

6. Send a letter to your district superintendent officially requesting a structure change and the convening of a Charge (Church) Conference.

7. The Committee on Nominations and Lay Leadership assembles to nominate new leaders illustrating new leadership criteria and structure.

8. The congregation's Charge Conference, preferably one convened as a Church Conference, is called with proper notice to approve:

• New structure

• Nominations

• A founding set of guiding principles that the new board is authorized to adapt to meet the ministry and missional needs of the church.

9. Congregational vote of the Charge or Church Conference. Once approved, all existing administrative teams cease to exist as separate bodies (this does not include ministry teams) on a certain date set by the Charge Conference. The responsibilities and authority of the constituent bodies will rest in the new board.

10. First meeting of the new board. Elect a trustee chair, orient the board on the guiding principles, and approve a board covenant.

STEP 1: Know your Why

The previous chapter outlined the importance of being intentional about your *why*. Continue to clarify and articulate your change using the motivating factors from Chapter 1: Efficiency, Alignment, Missional Focus, and Accountability. As you talk with your leadership and the congregation, we encourage you to also listen to your membership and your leaders. Use the chart on page 26-27 to build a draft time-line. Add in your town halls and listening session along with any preliminary approval steps unique to your congregation, conference, or denominational polity.

STEP 2: Preliminary DS Consultation

Your District Superintendent (DS) is also your district's mission strategist. For reasons connected to Disciplinary accountability, legal requirements, and to maintain alignment with the district missional plans and annual conference policies, consult with your DS before you really begin the process of moving toward simplified, accountable leadership structure, and then at every stage of the process leading up to and including the Charge Conference in which you seek approval to change structures. Your conference or DS may have specific requirements for congregational governance that you will want to follow. For instance, one of my (Blake's) fellow District Superintendents in Arkansas requires that churches transitioning to simplified structure continue to maintain a separate Pastor-Parish Relations Committee, so you will want to be sure to include any of those unique district or conference requirements early in your conversations.

If your DS is not familiar with the concept of a simplified, accountable leadership structure, you may want to provide her or him with a copy of this book. Many superintendents are just now learning the value of a simplified, account-able leadership structure, and may be a little nervous that traditional checks and balances are missing, so have some patience and be prepared to help educate your DS on the model. We actually suggest a minimum of two points of communication with your DS. First, have a preliminary conversation about the concept and scope of the possible new structure. When you seek preliminary approval from your DS, include the following items:

- Share your missional reasons for a possible structure change.

- List the names and roles of lay officers involved in the discussion up to this point.

- Share which Disciplinary administrative committees you believe will be incorporated into the governing Lead-ership Team. While this may, of course, change as your church leadership wrestles with the possibilities and options, your DS may have particular recommendations or requirements so that your church's structure may be approved.

- Share your proposed time-line for the structure change.

Please understand that your DS may respond with a "not yet." This could be due to her or his personal discomfort with the model itself, an awareness of relational or accountability issues in the congregation that might make "congregational health" a higher priority, or the DS may know that a change in pastoral leadership is coming soon, and the congregation may not have enough bandwidth for a simultaneous structure change and an announced pastoral transition.

STEP 3: Communicate with the Congregation

After this preliminary approval, you will need to be intentional in communicating with the congregation. Communication is key in discernment. Careful, comprehensive planning for upcoming conversations is crucial. Preparing the congregation is not only about "selling" a new structure or even "selling" a new set of leadership behaviors based on accountable leadership. Make sure to provide space for two-way communication so that the congregation can have ownership over the final result. Create opportunities to talk about the *why* first. Then move onto the "what" and "how." Use contextually appropriate gatherings, such as town hall meetings, along with private and group conversations with key leaders and constituencies (especially those who will perceive the change as a loss in power, prestige, or access).

Invite the congregation into multiple opportunities to hear about the proposed changes and to ask questions. Name the fears. Don't shy away from the concerns. If you can name them, you are then able to talk about them openly. Don't try to paint an "all is rosy" picture about the change. Name some of the potential challenges and how the church will navigate the challenges. Provide multiple opportunities for circles of conversations to inform people and create feedback loops.

For members who have been United Methodists for a long time, the "loss" of the Discipline-mandated administrative committees operating as separate and independent bodies can be perceived as a power grab, a loss of Methodist identity, or a loss of important checks-and-balances. Even in the healthiest of churches, a proposal to reduce the size of the leadership may be met with suspicion. Lack of excellent communication and complete transparency at this early point of discussion will destroy the trust the leadership team will need to transition the structure and to lead with a simplified, accountable leadership model.

STEP 4: Discernment and Structure

Ultimately, leaders must discern if it is the right time for the church to move through a structural change. If the feedback from most of your congregation is fear, you may need to work on overcoming those fears. You may need to practice better communication channels for a year before changing structure. You may have to work on transparency for a period of time before the congregation can trust the change. You may need to provide some overview training on simplified structure and accountable leadership before people can understand the proposed changes.

Use the congregational feedback, this book, and a careful study of the *United Methodist Book of Discipline* (or other denominational polity guide) to build your model for a simplified, accountable leadership structure. Remember that ministry teams and committees will continue to exist; it is primarily the administrative and strategic functions of governance that will be moved into the board.

STEP 5: Guiding Principles and Policy Audit

Your current church council or administrative board should approve the creation of a temporary task force to create a draft set of founding guiding principles (more on this in Chapter 6). The current chairs, or representatives, of the disciplinary committees (staff/pastor parish relations, finance, trustees) should probably be a part of the team, along with a member who is gifted at reading and studying policies. While the founding set of guiding principles are designed to evolve and be adapted by your new leadership board, take time to set some boundaries and ground rules. This founding set of guiding principles will be voted on along with the structure. This task force will need to read this book and have a thorough understanding of the work they are being tasked to provide.

Another assignment for this task force is to begin preparing updates for all existing congregational policies (personnel, facility, finance, safe sanctuary endowment, etc.) so that the policies will be in compliance with proposed structure. For instance, I (Blake) worked with a congregation that had a twenty-year-old endowment policy that named a certain number of representatives from trustees, council on ministries, and the administrative board, which was difficult since none of the three committees currently existed separately by that name. They needed a ninety percent vote (!) of a church conference to update their policy document. Similarly, I have seen personnel policies that include termination appeals systems that allow terminated employees to ask the church council to overturn a staff/parish relations committee decision. All these policies need a careful reading to discover inconsistencies with the new proposed structure.

Depending on your incorporation status, you may also need to update your by-laws with your state's Secretary of State office to reflect a change in governance structures. If your congregation has a member who serves as the church attorney or chancellor, this might be one of those situations where she or he needs to take a look at the documents before final approval. Some conferences have district chancellors who might be able to look at your documents, especially for smaller churches. Ask your district superintendent about specific guidelines or Disciplinary interpretation.

STEP 6: DS Approval

Once you have discerned your congregation is ready to move into simplified structure with accountable leadership, the pastor and church council must write a letter to his/her district superintendent requesting the alternative structural modification and an explanation of your missional purpose that undergirds the change. For this formal step of DS approval:

- Reference *BOD* paragraph 247.2, the passage that allows a church to "modify the organizational plans" of the congregation.

- Share the purpose, process, and time-line you used to present and communicate the simplified, accountable leadership model.

- The current Church Council/Administrative Board (not the pastor) should share the purpose for a structure change. We have seen too many situations where the pastor was the only one who understood the new structure.

- Outline your proposed simplified, accountable leadership model. List the Discipline-required roles and committees affected and share how (and by whom) those required administrative functions will be fulfilled. Include a founding set of guiding principles that the new Leadership Board will be allowed to adapt.

- Request permission to move forward with nominations for the new structure. Share your plan, process, and schedule for seeking nominations.

- Request that a Charge Conference approve the new slate of officers and the new structure (see Step 8). Name exactly which committees will make up the new Leadership Board, and clearly state the date (such as January 1) that the listed existing administrative committees will cease to exist as separate committees, the current committee members will vacate their positions, and all their responsibilities and authority (as stated in the *Book of Discipline*) will rest in the newly elected Leadership Team.

• Request that the Charge Conference be convened as a Church Conference to extend the vote to all professing members of the congregation, in order to "encourage broader participation by members of the church" (*BOD* paragraph 248).

STEP 7: Nominations Committee Prepares a Leadership Slate

The Committee on Nominations and Lay Leadership assembles to nominate new leaders illustrating new leadership criteria and structure. Chapter 5 will go into great detail on the types of leaders you will need to build your team. You are certainly looking to build a team with diverse perspectives, but you are not constituting a board made up of "representatives" of different ministries, such as the choir, the men's group, or that team that picks up groceries for the food pantry. You are looking for mature disciples who can set aside personal agendas or favorite ministries and lead the work of the whole church towards Christ's mission.

As part of the recruitment and orientation process, give your new board members a copy of this book. Operating as a simplified, accountable leadership board can be a bit disorienting to folks who have become comfortable in our inherited leadership structure of representatives reading committee reports.

Actually, now that the congregation knows a bit more

about accountable leadership and how the board will have both responsibility and the authority to live out the congregation's mission, you might find it easier to recruit new people. We have found that folks are often excited to serve on a team that will actually be able to lead! Some churches have used the opportunity of higher interest to have the nominations committee serve as an "interview team" culling through application (see Appendix E) of folks seeking to serve on the board.

STEP 8: Convene a Charge (Church) Conference

If the DS approves your request in Step 6, a Church Conference will be called in accordance with the *Book of Discipline* to vote on the new structure and a slate of nominations. Appendix F offers a sample of a simplified structure nominations committee report. Your DS may wish to separate these two items of business. For instance, she may wish to convene a called Church Conference to consider the new structure change in the summer and then allow the slate of nominations for the new structure to be a part of the regular business of the annual Charge Conference in the autumn, with everything becoming official on January 1 of the new year.

You will need to state the change in governance clearly because there are legal and Disciplinary consequences to this change in structure. A motion might include a statement like: "All references to the Church Council, Board of Trustees, Staff/Pastor Parish Relations Committee, Endowment Committee, and Finance Committee, in all congregational policies as of _____ (date), and in all references in the *Book of Discipline of the United Methodist Church*, shall be understood to refer to the Leadership Board beginning _____ (date)."

STEP 9 Congregational Vote of the Charge or Church Conference.

After the Church Conference, and regardless of the outcome of the vote, the work has really just begun. If the vote was not favorable, there is much work to be done towards the healthiness of the church. If the vote is favorable, there will be much work towards moving through many technical as well as adaptive changes. Once approved, all existing administrative teams cease to exist as separate bodies (this does not include ministry teams) on a certain date set by the Charge Conference. The responsibilities and authority of the constituent bodies will rest in the new board.

STEP 10: First meeting of the new board.

See Chapter 6 for a whole list of items you will need to do as your new board gets started. You will need to elect a trustee chair, orient the board on the guiding principles, and discern a board covenant. You will also need to discuss how you really want to "do business" differently.

How can your agenda template encourage creativity and limit redundancy? How will your board stay focused on accountability and adaptive leadership when the daily grind of institutional management is distracting you from being a governing board?

One of the most difficult steps on the checklist is the communication process you will need to create and implement in order to build congregational trust. This is especially true in congregations with legacy congregational structures of the huge "Board of Stewards" quarterly meetings of fifty people or the bicameral Administrative

Board and Council on Ministry system that required those two governing committees to agree on everything before anything could be approved. In these models, accountability was expressed in quantitative terms of the huge percentage of members in a governing position instead of qualitatively through intentional accountable leadership processes (more on that in Chapter 3). If your church has these legacy structures, your people will certainly need a lot more education than a PowerPoint slide of a smaller organizational chart. You will need to educate, to build trust, to acknowledge suspicions, and to stay missional.

Below is a checklist to communicate the shift into simplified structure for your congregation.

Checklist for Communicating the Change

- Communicate! Communicate! Communicate!

- Listen! Listen! Listen! Two-way communication is an imperative.

- Lead with the *why* and then follow with the "what" and "how." If your only *why* is the smaller membership of the church, and a simplified board sounds easier with smaller numbers, you are approaching this change for the wrong reason. Changing the structure without changing behaviors means that your church will keep on doing what it has always done, but now with less voices around the leadership table. Keep your *why* missional!

- Stay connected and acknowledge the sense of loss for members deeply invested in the former or current structure.

- Be transparent, and be sure that all communications are designed in a way that builds trust.

CHAPTER THREE

Accountable Leadership Must Come First

From Blake:

I remember one of the most frustrating planning meetings of my ministry. It was the first meeting of the team to set our plans for the year, and a key leader would bring preliminary copies for everyone. What we received was disheartening. We each received a single sheet of paper, with the date three years ago printed at the top and a listing, January through December, of events. For each item, January through December, the printed dates three years ago were marked out and last year's date handwritten in beside each event. Additionally, last year's "preliminary" schedule was marked out and instead the current year was scribbled beside all the other years' updates. It was planning by photocopy!

In a contemporary church culture where we often do ministries *"just because ..."* (i.e. *just because* it sounds charitable, or *just because* Mrs. Matriarch wants to, or *just because* we always have done it that way), accountable leadership feels radical. Rarely do we create ministries with the transformational impact in mind and work backwards from that goal. However, both of your authors are formed by Wesleyan Christianity, and so accountability is part of our history. The early Methodist societies always kept count of members, money, and ministry. While we may think of Annual Conference as a business meeting, revival, or equipping event, its origins were as an annual accountability tool: how many new class meetings and bands (small groups) were formed, how many souls were reached for Christ, and how well were our traveling preachers leading the expansion of the Church into new territory for new people? We can recover that meaningful accountability today. That is if we are willing to start with our end in mind (impactful transformation) and then work backwards from our goal while creating systems of accountability under the stewardship of the new Leadership Board.

Accountable Leadership

I (Kay) always offer this caution in training on simplified, accountable structure:

> **Some** churches can move to simplified, accountable structure and be effective. **All** churches should practice accountable leadership.

> **No** church should move to simplified structure without accountable leadership practices.

I have found the book, *Winning on Purpose*, by John Edmund Kaiser to be an invaluable tool in simplifying structure. In working with pastors and churches across the nation, it has become very apparent that most churches do not practice accountability. In fact, some churches are quite resistant in enacting accountability practices. In my work with churches, if they are unwilling to adapt to accountability practices, I do not recommend simplification. If accountable leadership is not put into place along with simplification, it will simply not be conducive to a healthy organization. In fact, it can quite possibly create the opposite. Accountability can be put into action with simplification, but simplification without accountability is bad news!

Accountability is marrying responsibility and authority. In other words, accountable leadership is when a person is given the responsibility and authority for a job or project and his/her supervisor holds the person accountable for the intended and agreed upon outcome. Accountability often gets a bad rap because it is often confused with blaming. But blaming is really quite different than accountability. While accountability connects responsibility and authority, blaming usually occurs when someone had responsibility but no actual authority or capacity to fulfill the expectations.

Accountable leadership in a church is quite simple in concept, but much less readily practiced. Here are some other great reasons to consider implementing accountable leadership into the life of your church beginning with the board/council:

1. Marries responsibility and authority with accountability

2. Promotes church unity

3. Functions on a high level of trust

4. Decisions are made very quickly

5. Mission/Vision fulfillment is the driving force ... not management (or maintenance)

6. Goals and objectives of ministries can be adjusted as needed.

The first entity that a leadership board must hold accountable is themselves. As the governing and strategic board, it has both the responsibility and the authority to lead. The governing board is accountable to God to fulfill Christ's mission and to use its authority to hold the rest of the church accountable to Christ's mission as well. The leadership board is accountable to Christ (the owner of the church) for the church being faithful in fulfilling its mission of making disciples of Jesus Christ for the transformation of the world.

If we only talk accountability, but are unable or unwilling to live it, it will never work! Accountability is simple! Here are the steps to hold people accountable:

S	=	Set Expectations
I	=	Invite Commitment
M	=	Measure Progress
P	=	Provide Feedback
L	=	Link to Consequences
E	=	Evaluate Effectiveness.

Accountable leadership depends on clarity of roles. One reason we advocate for simplified, accountable structure in congregations is that the complexity of offices and committees creates blurry lines of authority that undermine accountability. Churches with no clarity around authority often argue so much about who "gets" to make a decision that often the decision is made too late, or is undermined at the first chance. John Edmund Kaiser's *Winning on Purpose* (pages 46 & 107), has deeply influenced our understanding of the roles for the various positions for accountable leadership:

- **Board/Council** = Role is governance (fiduciary, generative, and strategic work)

- **Pastor** = Role is leading the people into the mission field through communicating God's mission and vision

- **Staff** (paid & unpaid) = Role is managing the day-to-day ministry

- **Members** = Role is ministering to the church, the neighborhood, and the larger world.

Understanding these roles is vitally important in moving into both simplification and accountability. This proper understanding is critical in the shift of becoming more effective, efficient, and faithful as a church. Most churches we work with have steep learning curves when it comes to understanding these roles. The biggest shift most churches need to make is the board/council moving from <u>managing to governing</u>.

We often share with congregations we work with that if the board/council is not talking about and monitoring its effectiveness in its mission of making disciples, then no one is monitoring it. What we pay attention to is what we deem important. If all we are paying attention to are such things as the calendar, the building, and the money, we lose sight of the most important reason we exist – Jesus' mission! When we are not paying attention to our effectiveness in reaching the mission, we most assuredly drift away from the mission!

Accountable Leadership Cycle

In our book, *IMPACT! Reclaiming the Call of Lay Ministry*, (pages 112-113), we shared about what accountable leadership looks like in a local church, by starting with your missional purpose as a congregation and then doing the necessary discernment, planning, implementation, evaluation and reflective learning:

Assessment, evaluation, and reflection are critically important to a healthy governance model when practicing accountable leadership. We must become proficient with assessment at every level. The board is accountable to Christ for the church living its mission of making disciples. The pastor is accountable to the board for the church's annual goals and living into its vision of God's preferred future for how it uniquely makes disciples. The staff (paid and unpaid ministry leaders) are accountable to the pastor for the day-to-day ministry, with the pastor ensuring that the ministries are aligned with the church's annual goals. Constant and consistent evaluation at all levels is critical to enable the church to assess its fruitfulness and remain in alignment of its purpose/mission.

Finally, the board needs to take time to reflect on ministries and their effectiveness. Accountability is not about blaming, but it's certainly about learning. An organization that never reflects on their work never learns or adapts. A word of warning: Evaluation and accountability are key, but please know that this is an incredibly difficult shift to live into because it will take persistence and patience.

This chart offers a graphic representation of the accountable leadership cycle:

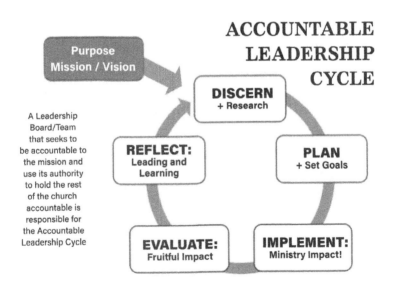

While a board may not have a direct hand in every step of this process, the governing board should be engaged by ensuring that others are held to an appropriate level of accountability. While the board will not be planning the ministry or the event themselves, they can, for example, be very clear about the goals of particular ministries. Similarly, the first set of ministry or event evaluations may happen at a staff or ministry team level.

Setting goals for ministries not only creates a compelling purpose that will attract more congregational energy, it also reminds everyone of our purpose for a specific ministry. For instance, if we know that a goal of a neighborhood carnival is to get names and do excellent follow-up, we will organize the ministry very differently than if we didn't include that evangelistic element. What might have been just a nice event for the neighborhood becomes a disciple-making bridge event to build relationships. Goals matter.

Strategies matter, too! Strategies are the activities and ministries that occur from day to day in the life of the congregation. Sometimes those activities are strategic, but most often they are "just what we do because that is what we have always done." What we do day-to-day in the life of our church must align to our mission of making disciples. Strategies are the reflection of our "doing ministry" in connection with our purpose - our mission. When the simplified, accountable structure (the leadership team/board) sets the annual goals of the church to help the church live into their mission and vision, the pastor then works with the staff (paid and unpaid ministry team leaders) to align the strategies (the day-to-day ministries) that will help the church live into the mission of making disciples. The pastor holds the staff accountable, and the board holds the pastor accountable.

From Blake:

When I coach congregations, one of the questions I ask to determine how committed the leadership is to accountability is: "Tell me about the last few ministries you intentionally shut down." Congregations often clutter up their calendars with busy work, not Kingdom work, thinking a full calendar is a sign of missional impact. Meanwhile, the abundance of programs struggle to find enough volunteers to serve, soak up budget resources, exhaust staff, distract the congregation from larger goals, and leave no space for new endeavors that could actually capture people's missional imaginations. Until church leaders are willing to make the hard call and conduct funeral services for worn out or distracting ministries (well done, good and faithful ministry!), accountable leadership will always remain theoretical.

The governance responsibilities of the board are three-fold: fiduciary, generative, and strategic. Fiduciary responsibility speaks to the appropriate care and management of the church's assets such as real estate, cash, human resources, and investments. Generative responsibility includes being proactive in planning and guiding the organization into its future, such as team building, creatively asking new questions, and seeking out new opportunities to make disciples. Generative work is about the proper application of the church's mission and vision as an organization and a movement of God. Strategic responsibilities would include making sure there is proper planning and goal setting to align with the mission and vision.

An Accountable Leadership Conversation

From Kay:

I was once coaching a church living into their first year of simplified, accountable structure. It was one of those situations where both the new leadership board and the pastor were all-in and ready to embrace this new leadership style. We journeyed through the strategic planning retreat setting, goals were set, and core values were articulated. The pastor had worked with staff to create the strategies to ensure the goals were met. The budget to support the strategies was approved. The stage was set and I attended one of their leadership board meetings to hold them accountable for the process of living into simplified, accountable leadership.

Here is a sampling of some of the conversation that occurred that evening:

Board chair: *Pastor, tell us how each of the church goals is progressing?*

Pastor: *Goal one: the bridge event had four hundred people in attendance. We collected two hundred forty names. The connection team was able to engage in the first step of the follow-up system with just under one hundred of those attending.*

Goal two: the worship design team has been assembled. They have had one training session. We will have another training session next month. The following month we will begin to work on the following six months of worship planning. I feel I am missing the perspective of a new believer on the team and will be praying on who might be a good fit for that team. Do you have any suggestions?

Board member: *Pastor, things are really progressing well on the church goals. I believe you also had some personal goals that you asked for us to hold you accountable for. Those were a date night with your spouse twice a month, taking Fridays as your sabbath, and living into a personal health plan. Tell us how each of those are going for you.*

This was simply amazing blessing to witness. So many struggle with this accountability as it is seen as a negative.

It often feels more like blaming than graceful and missional. Yet during this encounter that I was privileged to observe, it was the power of accountability leadership demonstrated at the church and personal level. All felt empowered. All felt they were part of this collaborative, supportive team that was collectively making a difference in the life of the church and in the life of the pastor. When accountable leadership is embraced and fully practiced, it is a powerfully positive force.

Coaching Questions as you consider Accountable Leadership

How ready is your church to practice accountable leadership? Use these coaching questions to reflect on your readiness:

1. How does your current board or church council hold ministries accountable to the mission and vision of the church? For instance, do you require evaluations, study metrics, or spend time assisting ministry leaders in reflecting upon the purpose of ministries? When was the last time your church intentionally shut down (or put on evaluative "hiatus") a ministry for being ineffective?

2. How do your committees and ministry teams utilize your mission, vision, and goals when you need to make decisions or prioritize items in your budget? If the mission statement is read at the start of the meeting before the prayer, but never brought up as your team discerns next steps or influences your spending decisions, then is it actually being used for guidance, or is it just a marketing tag-line?

3. How effectively is your accountable leadership practiced

currently at all levels (board, pastor, staff, teams)? If we do not routinely inquire about what is being accomplished and hold one another accountable for moving forward towards our goals, we may be encountering an accountability crisis.

CHAPTER FOUR

Structuring the Leadership

It was a meeting like most church board meetings. You walk into the room, pick up your copy of the minutes and financial reports and take a seat. The pastor opened in prayer. Then the reporting started ... it seemed like it would never end. There were endless reports about what we had already done being read directly word for word from a report that would become part of the minutes. If there were decisions to be made, it was either a rubber stamp approval or a referral to another committee. No one was quite sure who really had a vote so everyone voted. There was never a mention of how the church was aligning itself (or not) to the mission of disciple making. There was no mention of annual goals and progress. No one had a clue about baptisms or professions of faith. We were simply there to hear reports and rubber stamp any decision brought before the group. Some leave the meeting feeling like it was a big waste of time. It seemed like we were just going through the motions. And, the meetings have gone this way for decades ... or more.

Does that sound like any church board meeting you have ever attended? If so, allow us to give you hope that there is another way and what we believe is a more faithful an effective method to lead churches.

Most churches have traditionally been structured with four administrative committees. Those committees include finance, trustees, staff/pastor parish relations committee (S/PPRC) and the board/council. Each team functions separately. The interesting part is the difference from church to church in how the committees relate (or not) to one another and how they relate to the pastor. Those differences would denote how the structure functions, and the chain of command. This is commonly demonstrated in an organizational chart. When consulting with congregations, it is always a fun exercise to ask the leaders of a church to sketch their organizational chart. First, most congregational leaders have never really considered mapping their structure, let alone creating an actual chart on paper. Secondly, most times there are a variety of charts presented to us. Most often we are handed at least six to eight different and conflicting charts from the same church. Sometimes leaders report not even knowing where to start. No wonder we struggle with our current structure! We must have a common understanding as to how each committee relates to each other, who is responsible for what, how we function together and separately, and how the pastor relates to each committee or team.

In addition to all challenges mentioned above, another challenge is when a church finds itself with a huge number of positions to fill, but a limited number of people to fill them. Once all the official *administrative* committees are filled (or perhaps filled partially), there are simply not enough people to fill the *ministry* positions. We seemed to place a higher emphasis on filling the administrative positions first, thus leaving a small percentage for the ministry. Through this practice, we tend to focus on our internal affairs more than we focus on doing ministry to reach new people for Jesus Christ – our very mission! This is one of the many reasons why we have an abundance of internally focused churches struggling to be vital in their communities.

It is because of the confusion, the common likelihood of silo-ing committees, the complexity, and the cumbersome nature of operating in the structure created in and for the 1960's that more and more churches are moving to a more streamlined and efficient structure. While the restructuring option was provided as an opportunity to streamline for small churches, large churches were among the first to adopt the simplified structure.

In the United Methodist Church's *Book of Discipline* (*BOD*), there is a provision to structure your church uniquely for missional purposes. Below is an excerpt from paragraph 247.2 in the 2016 *Book of Discipline*:

> *The charge conference, the district superintendent, and the pastor shall organize and administer the pastoral charge and churches according to the policies and plans herein set forth. When the membership size, program scope, mission resources, or other cir-cumstances so require, the charge conference may, in consultation with and upon the approval of the district superintendent, modify the organizational plans, provided that the provisions of ¶ 243 are observed.*

And paragraph 243 reads:

> *¶ 243. Primary Tasks – The local church shall be organized so that it can pursue its primary task and mission in the context of its own community – reaching out and receiving with joy all who will respond; encouraging people in their relationship with God and inviting them to commitment to God's love in Jesus Christ; pro-viding opportunities for them to seek strengthening and growth in spiritual formation; and supporting them to live lovingly and justly in the power of the Holy Spirit as faithful disciples.*

A church must still fulfill the requirements for the responsibilities of finance, trustees (property), and staff parish relations (personnel) as well as the board/council. However, the way those responsibilities are fulfilled can be done in more effective and efficient methods that reflect more modern systems.

Because of the general wording in the *BOD* paragraph 247, there are a variety of ways to streamline structure. There is no one way that is right or perfect. But as we have walked alongside hundreds of congregations to implement this, we will share best practices based on the collection of those experiences. You will need to take local context and values into consideration when establishing the new structure. Our recommendation, whenever possible and as a best practice, is to do a pure, full model of simplification. This means that all four administrative teams would be rolled into one single board. Technically, the trustees, finance committee, and S/PPRC all still exist, but they are all the Leadership Team.

However, there are times when this full-model simplification is just not possible. For example, sometimes there is just too much of a political powerhouse in place with trustees, and so the trustee committee may need to operate separately for a while until more trust can be built up. Likewise, some congregations have an endowment committee that reports to their church council or to the trustees.

Endowments often have complex governing documents that may require multiple steps to include their functions in a simplified governing board, so it may be best to simplify the rest of the functions, and have a time-line to include the endowment responsibilities. If the endowment is not a separately incorporated entity, as a best practice we recommend disbanding the endowment committee and bringing this responsibility under the umbrella of the governing board.

Do not allow complicated politics to keep you from moving forward. You have two options if this occurs. The first option is to work for a while on training, communication, and practicing accountability to create conditions that allow complete simplification to take place. The second option is to gradually move into complete simplification over a two or three-year period.

The primary drawback to this "step-in" method is that it creates a large amount of role confusion on the part of the leaders and the congregation, and the church has to be very intentional to maintain Disciplinary-approved processes during the transition.

How to Structure

First, a common mistake is describing simplified structure is that "we got rid of all of our committees." Actually, all your committees still exist and together, all their combined responsibilities constitute the authority of the new leadership board. In other words, the Leadership Board IS the Finance Committee and IS the Staff/Pastor Parish Committee and IS the Trustees and IS the Church Council. Nothing in the *Book of Discipline* is ignored or removed. Instead, the functions, roles, and responsibilities of each of the constituent committees are all placed upon your new board.

To move into the most simplified structure, you will need nine to thirteen members. Because nine is the standard sized committee required by the *BOD* for trustees, finance, and SPRC, this is the minimum size for a simplified structure. If your church has a chartered United Methodist Men or United Methodist Women and someone from those groups requests to be on the Board, you may need someone from those groups serving on the new structure. You will also need a youth, lay leader, lay member of Annual Conference, and chair. Keep in mind, members on the new structure can serve in multiple roles. This single committee then serves all the functions listed in the *BOD* for the Committees on Finance, Staff Parish Relations, Trustees, and Council.

It is recommended that the board chair be elected as the trustee chair at the board's first meeting each January. Likewise, we recommend the board/council chair be named by the Nominations Committee as the staff/pastor parish relations liaison to the district superintendent. This recommendation comes from some difficult experiences when the board chair was not the district superintendent's contact.

As a DS, I (Blake) have gotten conflicting requests from a chair and a separate SPR liaison, which muddied up the *Disciplinary* waters, legally speaking. Information was coming in from someone on the board rather than the chair and information was not necessarily shared or disseminated with the rest of the members of the committee. Therefore, it is deemed a best practice for all outside coordination or correspondence be done through the board chair, serving in her or his dual capacity as the S/PPRC chair.

To comply with the *BOD* and to keep the team fresh and accountable, you will still need to place members into three classes (i.e. Class of 2020, Class of 2021, Class of 2022). Approximately one-third of the board will then rotate off each year and new people will be seated. This allows for both continuity, historical preservation, and including new leaders each year.

Example of board/council roster:

Class of 2020   Class of 2021

John Jones, T/F/SPR   Jennifer Jackson, T/F/SPR/C

Carol Clark, T/F/SPR/LM   Ben Black, T/F/SPR/LL

Larry Lewis, T/F/SPR   Yolanda Youngperson, F/SPR/Y

Class of 2022

Sue Smith, T/F/SPR/UMW

David Dent, T/F/SPR/UMM

Debbie Duncan, T/F/SPR

Key

T-Trustee	F-Finance
SPR – Staff Parish Relations	C-Chair
LL-Lay Leader	LM-Lay Member to Annual Conference
UMM-United Methodist Men	UMW-United Methodist Women
Y-Youth	

In addition to this example, you can find a complete sample nominations report in the appendix.

The Organizational Chart

On the following page, you will find a chart that outlines a simplified structure with accountable leadership. This chart illustrates clear lines of authority, responsibility, and accountability. It provides clarity for who reports to who and the role for each. Study the chart. What shifts will need to be made to live into this new structure? What communication needs to occur? What training and coaching is needed? Identify potential learning curves at all levels. What resourcing is needed to overcome those learning curves?

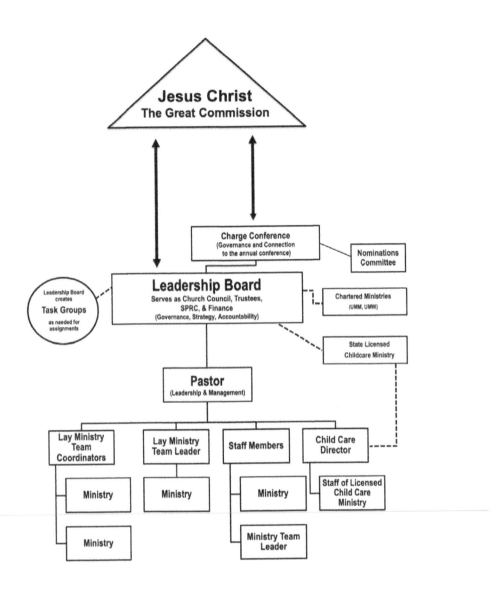

Note on Ministry Teams

Dan Entwistle, the Managing Executive Director for Programs and Ministries at the United Methodist Church of the Resurrection, uses the excellent metaphor of a bicycle to describe the difference between the strategic work of a governing board and the mobilization work of ministry teams. Imagine a bicycle. There are two major points of interaction with every bike. You have your handlebars and your pedals. The handlebars are for steering. Through the handlebars, you set the direction you want to go. The pedals are for locomotion to create the power that takes the bicycle where you are steering.

A bike with no pedals goes nowhere. A bike without a working set of handlebars will land you in a ditch. The Leadership Board's job is to do the **steering** – to set the direction via strategic visioning, mission alignment, accountability, and administration. For ministry **mobilization**, to actually get to the place Christ is calling your church, you are going to need some pedals. Mobilization is the work of ministry teams.

Ministry teams work very differently than elected leaders on a governing committee. Members of ministry teams are not nominated and elected for specific terms like the members of a council/board. Instead they are selected based on their gifts and passion for a particular area of ministry, with no predetermined length of service. They are identified, recruited, and equipped by staff (paid or unpaid), team leaders, and/or the pastor.

Teams may last only as long as a particular project, or may serve on an ongoing basis, with members joining and moving off the team throughout its life. They could be led by a volunteer or a staff member and should ultimately be accountable to the oversight of the pastor. It is suggested that a move to simplified structure include changing the names of assorted ministry committees, such as "Worship Committee," to a name that more appropriately describes a ministry team's defined work such as Worship Planning Team, Worship Design Advisory Team, Praise Team, or Worship and Hospitality Team. This helps to define the expectations for team members and also brings clarity to the differences between the governance of committees (steering) versus the ministry of teams (mobilization).

The Work of Trustees

Let us take a moment and talk specifically about work teams for trustees. This is another area where churches get tripped up in moving to the simplified structure. In many churches, trustees have been tapped, practiced, or labeled as being the people who perform the actual hands-on work on the building and grounds. They maintain the grounds, change the light bulbs in the sanctuary, and fix the running toilet. They certainly take care of the fiduciary responsibilities of the trustees (such as property insurance, facility policies, lease agreements, filing bylaws and articles of incorporation with the state), but in most cases the majority of their time and energy is spent on building and parsonage repairs and maintenance.

This care-taking need obviously does not go away in the new model. Our church property still needs to be maintained. To use the bicycle metaphor, there is still pedaling needed. In our experience, the people who enjoy hands-on work do not necessarily enjoy the fiduciary work and attending meetings. The hands-on work is their ministry using their gifts! Our recommendation and experience as a best practice is to have a Building Maintenance Team. Give this team the authority and responsibility to care for repairs and maintenance within healthy parameters set by the board.

(See suggested sample Guiding Principles in Chapter 6 for examples of parameters.) This practice allows this team to go about the business of building maintenance without being bogged down in the administrative and fiduciary responsibilities that are now being handled by the board, such as handling matters of policy and insurance.

When creating a Building Maintenance Team, you will want to select a trusted team leader and give her or him some authority to select team members as needed. Because it is a ministry team, and not a committee, term limits are not an issue and giftedness can be the primary criteria. This is a ministry team and would most likely report to a staff person or to the board. You will also want to specify the limits of the team's spending authority in your Guiding Principles (see Chapter 6 for more on Guiding Principles).

Keep a Separate Nominations Committee

The Committee on Nominations and Leadership Development nominates members of only two committees: the governing board and Nominations. The *BOD* does not allow the duties of the Nominations Committee to be rolled into the new simplified council/board, so it will continue to exist and serve. For the most part, these will be the only two standing committees. The only exception for this would be if there is a separately incorporated church entity such as an Endowment Committee. Note: If the Endowment Committee is not a separately incorporated entity, the responsibilities will roll into the board's responsibilities and governess.

The Committee on Nominations and Leadership Development is to have no more than nine members, not including the pastor, who is the chair of the committee. Members are placed in three classes.

Remember, ministry teams are recruited and equipped by the pastor and staff. The ministry teams are all "pedaling together" to accomplish the objectives driven by the church goals. Teams are created and discontinued as needed to accomplish the ministry. There is no need for standing teams in name only (like we practiced in the old model of structure) whose membership is elected as an annual slate proposed by the Nominations Committee. Of course, you will still need some standing teams for such ministry tasks as hospitality, children/youth ministry, missions, building and grounds, and worship design. These teams do not need to be elected and placed in your formal nominations report. However, you might want to include the team membership list as an addendum for historical reasons, or to help publicize their function and contact information.

Structuring for a multiple-church-point charge or cooperative parish

In the United Methodist Church, smaller congregations are often linked together as a multi-point circuit, a cooperative parish, or as a single charge. In cases where your congregation is considering moving toward a simplified, accountable leadership structure, but you are linked with a congregation that follows a more traditional structure, be sure to include both your district superintendent in the conversation about the conference's expectations for sharing the work of the staff/pastor relations committee (S/PPRC). If the churches are considered to be a single charge, it is appropriate to have a single S/PPRC made up of members from each church to represent the interests and ministry of both congregations.

One solution is for the nominating committee to assign a few members from your Leadership Board to be representatives on the combined S/PPRC (including the lay leader), and to have those assignments approved as part of your charge conference.

In Cooperative Parishes, wide latitude is provided for structuring the relationship between multiple congregations. Your Leadership Board may serve as the congregation's S/PPRC and relate to the other S/PPRCs in the parish, or a separate S/PPRC may need to be created by your Charge Conference. Your district superintendent will certainly have some expectations around these options.

Additionally, in some flavors of the cooperative parish, there are options to create a single parish or charge council to oversee the ministries of all the worshiping and ministry locations. If all the constituent congregations have experience in the simplified, accountable leadership structure, you may decide to "go simple" for the entire parish with a single governing board that is made up of members from all the ministry sites.

Rules to Remember

All the Disciplinary requirements and limitations of each of the new Leadership Board's constituent committees remains in effect. Rules to remember:

1. A separate **Nominations Committee**, chaired by the Pastor, is required because the Board cannot self-nominate.

2. You will need **nine to fifteen** members. Board members serve a **three-year term**. The Lay Leader and Lay Delegate are exempt from the three-year term. After being off the Board for a year, the person can roll back onto the Board if elected. SPRC and Trustees have minimum and maximum limits on the number of members, so (depending on your Leadership Team's size and composition), a few members of the Leadership Team may be barred as voting members of some of the constituent committees. For instance, there is a limit of nine on Trustees. There is also a limit of eleven on SPRC, counting Lay Leader and a Lay Member of Annual Conference.

3. Pay attention to *Disciplinary* **conflicts of interest**. Household members cannot serve on the Board together. If it cannot be avoided, the family members may need to excuse themselves from the room or not vote on issues with potential conflict of interest. Staff and family of staff cannot serve on the Board because of SPRC membership restrictions (plus it is simply good ethics!).

4. Trustee Requirements: During the first meeting at the beginning of each new year, the Board will elect a Trustee Chair to satisfy the corporate resolution requirement. It is recommended the Board Chair serve as the Trustee Chair, if the Board chair is one of the Trustees. The Leadership Board, serving as the Trustees, is also the legal Board of Directors. All Board members who serve as Trustees must be over eighteen. The Trustee membership rule of minimum one-third laymen and one-third lay women remains in effect. The Pastor cannot be a Trustee.

5. Even though the restructuring occurs, **ministry teams** are still needed and in place. Fewer people on the Board means more people are available to do ministry. Simplifying structure is the combining of the four administrative teams of the Council, Trustees, Finance, and SPR Committees. The nurture, outreach, and witnessing ministries continue their disciple-making work.

6. The concept of a Leadership Board is **designed to increase accountability and alignment** for the whole church towards its holistic mission, not be a place for ministry representatives to negotiate "turf." Members of the Board only represent and lead the whole church, not a particular interest group or ministry.

7. While the Leadership Board **may designate specialists** (such as finance specialists) from the membership of their Board, the whole Board, *in toto*, serves as the finance committee, Trustees, etc., not just the designated specialists.

8. The small number of governance officers on the Leadership Team **requires huge trust and congregation-wide accountability**. It is HIGHLY RECOMMENDED that you describe your future Charge Conference as being "The Leadership Board, Nominations Committee, and all clergy who hold their charge conference in the congregation." It would also greatly help build trust, accountability, and transparency if your governing documents adopt a recommendation that asks the District Superintendent to convene all Charge Conferences as Church Conferences to allow all professing members to vote on matters. This allows the larger congregation to have a say in nominations and hold the Leadership Board accountable in the Board's role as the Charge Conference's executive committee.

9. Churches on **multi-point charges** will particularly need to take care to support and respect the organizational structure and ministry of one another's churches.

Specialists or "Representatives"

In the early years of churches converting to simplified structure, a common procedure was for the nominating committee to assign titles of specialists, which were sometimes called "representatives." Some still appreciate issuing titles and certain areas of responsibility for the areas of finance, trustees, and SPR.

There are pros and cons for titles or designees. The pros for giving members a title (for example "Trustee Representative"), is assigning specific and direct responsibility over a given area. There is then a go-to person as the congregation is accustomed to having. This is less of a learning curve for most congregations.

The cons of having titles is the three people having these titles many times still act as their own separate committee. Therefore, three people end up making important decisions in their work area that they really do not have any authority to do. It creates or reinforces working silos. Accountability and adaptive changes are harder to instill.

A common mistake is if the "representative" or "specialist" title is given to certain people on the board, there is a misperception that the sub-group of the board of those three representatives or specialists are now a mini-trustee, finance, or SPR team. The *BOD* requires a minimum number of people for these administrative committees. So not only are the three people working as the committee against the rules of the *BOD*, but only three people making decisions is not healthy for the church overall.

PROS of Having Specialist Titles:	CONS of having Specialist Titles:
• Assigning specific and direct responsibility over a given area creates an identifiable go-to person for members. • This is less of a learning curve for most congregations.	• The three people having these titles many times still act as their own separate committee, but now with only a couple of voices, robbing the larger Leadership Board of their responsibility and accountability. In these situations, three people end up making important decisions in their work area that they really do not have any authority to do, which is also a violation of the Discipline. • It creates or reinforces working silos. • Accountability and adaptive change are harder to instill.

Now let me (Kay) offer my personal bias based on working with hundreds of pastors and churches. (Of course, you are welcome to take it or leave it!) In working with numerous congregations and pastors, I highly recommend simplifying all the way (without specialist titles) if at all possible. In my experience, the churches that keep titles find it more difficult to operate in a renewed mode. By keeping titles, members of the new simplified board arrive to the meeting table envisioning their role as the "representative" for a set of issues (property, finances) or a particular committee (that no longer exists) instead of arriving at the meeting table as the gathered leaders of the entire congregation, seeking to engage the mission field for Jesus Christ. They are able to make the technical change of having fewer people at the table, but they are unable to make the adaptive shift to change the conversation and focus at the table. Old habits are not broken and instead perpetuate business as usual.

For there to be real transformation towards effectiveness, efficiency, and faithfulness towards the mission, the focus and conversation must evolve to live into the accountable leadership model. So, while your church may decide to have individual members of this committee serve as specialists or have particular assignments, please be sure to enforce the rule that only when the whole committee meets together can it serve the fiduciary responsibilities as the church's board. Specialists may bring recommendations, but all decisions will be made by the whole board together.

What's in a Name?

The conversation around the leadership table needs to change. To help the entire congregation understand there is a new structure, we strongly suggest changing the name of the board/council. For example, if you currently refer to your leadership team as an Administrative Council, change the name to the Church Board. Some other names used are: Vision Committee, Strategy Council, Ministry Table, Leadership Team/Board/Council. Changing the name helps draw a line in the sand that the church is doing a new thing!

If you are leaning heavily in articulating the difference between a committee/board (elected with a term of office) versus a team (selected and evolving membership with no particular term of service) using the language from earlier in this chapter, you will want to use Leadership Board or some other language that specifies that the governing board is an elected committee and not a ministry team.

Checklist for Structuring the Leadership

- Take the time to carefully discern your structure for your context. All the Disciplinary requirements for all the committees apply for your new board, which means that you will be flipping through multiple sections of the *Book of Discipline*. Structure by photocopy is not enough preparation. You will need to understand and communicate the mechanics of your new structure.

- Begin the transition towards building a maintenance team to handle day-to-day facility issues. Empower this team through the guiding principles. Even if this team reports to your board of trustees for several months while you are discerning your restructure plan, the maintenance team will have time to form and start working.

- Ensure you have a separate nominations and leadership development committee. Train them on the principles of simple accountable leadership.

- Choose an appropriate name for the newly formed leadership board.

CHAPTER FIVE

Choosing the Team

We have been there and we are sure you have likely been there, too. You have attended meetings that were irrelevant wastes of your time. You have attended very important meetings where people seemed to be elusive, unplugged, or maybe even absent. There are other times when people have a seat at the committee table because it is one of honor or prestige rather than responsibility, and they don't want to do the work.

You may have even worked on committees where committee members bring personal agendas to the table, or feel that their job at the leadership table is to "fight for their constituents" (a particular ministry team, the quilting circle, scouts, their beloved Sunday School or worship time, the endowment, etc.) when it comes time to prioritize staffing and finances. We have been there and we have all served on dysfunctional committees. Changing the structure and the agenda format are only part of the solution. We must also reconsider how we choose the people sitting at the table.

The Nominations Process

So, it is time for the annual gathering of the Committee

on Nominations and Leadership Development to meet to decide who should serve on which committees. Maybe your experience is different than ours, but most times it goes something like this, "Okay, so where is the latest copy of the church pictorial directory? Let's look through the pictorial to see if it will help us think of some new people. Who can we coerce to say yes? Who from the Nominations Committee should call so the nominee will most likely say yes?" That inherited process is more about filling slots with bodies. It is time for a new day with a new process for a new outcome!

The process actually starts months before the nominations begin. Notice, the official title of this committee is the Committee on Nominations _and Leadership_. We must have an intentional process of developing leaders. When churches have a leadership development process, it feeds the nominations process. I (Blake) have spent a couple of decades attending nominations committee meetings, and I quickly realized that there is a big difference between nominations meetings where we are all staring into the ceiling, trying to conjure up a name versus nominations meetings where we have profiles of engaged disciple-leaders on the table in front of us, and our job is to strategically manage the process of bringing leaders onto the team so we have a variety of gifts and perspectives.

In the leadership development process, potential leaders are invited into a journey that lasts from several weeks to several months with other potential leaders. This will be a time of discernment, faith development, and gift assessment led by the pastors and Nominations Committee. Remember, as the Nominations Committee, you are seeking to raise up three or four leaders for the board/council each year to fill vacancies for classes rolling off. In order to have these leaders prepared and ready for a commitment, you will likely need eight to ten leaders in the leadership development pathway. Some leaders will discern they are better suited to lead ministry teams rather than be a board member. Others might realize the timing for such a leadership covenant is not quite right. You might even have some go through the process that either do not finish, and/or the pastor discerns is not quite ready or equipped for leadership. In a reverse of the normal "fill the slot" mentality of many churches, some forward-thinking congregations even have a Nominations Committee application (see appendix for an example) and interview process in place for those seeking possible council/board membership.

In Kay's book, *Gear Up* (Abingdon Press 2017), you will find more resources and information on leadership development. Also check out our first bookd together, *IMPACT! Reclaiming the Call of Lay Ministry* (Market Square Books 2018). Future board members will need to understand that the goal of the leadership board is to lead the church in impacting the mission field, not simply to maintain the institution and keep their fellow Sunday School members happy.

What Are You Looking For?

Acts Chapter 6 and Paul's letters to Timothy and Titus offer some examples of qualifications for church leadership. Notice that the biblical qualifications focus on some timeless qualities like "full of the Spirit and wisdom," experience in personal "household" management, being "above reproach," and practicing of self-control in behaviors and relationships. Before anything else, church leaders need to be disciples of Jesus Christ. Church nominations committees often try to build committees for reasons unconnected to fulfilling the mission of Christ, such as attempting to please different constituencies, or out of concern that a wealthy member not feel excluded from decisions.

While we understand the political realities of leading a mostly volunteer institution, know that every person included on the board for non-missional reasons will distract your board from doing God's business. Even deeply devoted disciples may not be right for governance board work if they are unwilling to see beyond the ministry they are personally leading. For instance, I (Blake) remember working with a passionate leader of a feeding ministry. The leader raised thousands of dollars each month in in-kind gifts from grocery stores for distribution and worked with nonprofits and churches throughout the city. But, the leader was so passionate about her ministry that other ministries and groups, such as youth and children's ministries, were often pushed out of the way and their storage space "borrowed." This leader was so focused on one aspect of the church's ministry, the other areas were considered less important.

In business management, there is a metaphorical concept of leaving the frenetic activity of the dance floor and moving to the balcony where leaders can better see all the dynamics and figure things out (see Ronald Heifetz's and Marty Linsky's article "A Survival Guide for Leaders," in the June 2002 issue of the *Harvard Business Review)*. So, instead of getting a board filled with representatives of different groups or ministries, many of whom may wish to prioritize their own ministry above others, your nominations committee is seeking to identify, equip, and recruit leaders who can see the church from this "balcony perspective."

Your board leaders need to be completely dedicated to Jesus Christ, be growing as disciples, and be personally invested in the church's ministries. This is often a completely different process of identifying leadership than the practices we have inherited in church leadership. We can find experts in building, banking, or human resources most anywhere, and they can always be invited to participate on a project or task force. But to lead a church, it is of highest importance to have our most mature disciples at the table.

From Kay:

I once was working with a church who had a finance chair who did not attend church and gave absolutely no dollars to the ministry. I am still baffled how that type of thing can happen. A simplified, accountable leadership structure also has no spaces left over for honorific positions.

All board members are working members of the team, and the whole board must be committed to the church's mission. Church members may be extremely effective in business, pillars of the community, and show all the outward signs of "success," but if they are not dedicated disciples of Jesus Christ, then they need to keep on growing as members and not serve as leaders on your simplified, accountable structure board.

Take some time to consider the type of person the church needs as a leader. Think through some of these questions and discuss them in your nominations committee meeting:

- What are the characteristics, expectations, and behaviors that would be beneficial?

- Is there expectation that members of the board would be regular worship attenders, participants in a small group, serving periodically, have a regular prayer life, and a proportional giver (i.e. living and modeling their faith)?

72

- Is there an expectation that leaders would be available to attend most all board meetings?

- Would there be an expectation that leaders check their personal agendas at the door?

- Would there be an expectation that board members would be able to hold confidential information?

- Would the board member be able to openly support the decision of the board regardless of their personal feelings about the decision?

In addition to the people in your leadership pathway, the creation of a new leadership structure is an excellent opportunity to invite leaders who had sat on the sidelines. For many high-capacity leaders, the cumbersome old structure seen in most churches is a repellent. High-capacity leaders want to be challenged and make a difference, and the endless reports from endless committees was not attractive. A simplified and accountable leadership structure with a single board may be catnip to these high capacity leaders, so expand your search beyond the usual suspects and have meaningful conversations with these potential leaders. Whatever appropriate characteristics, expectations, and behaviors are named, potential leaders will discover these in the leadership development process. It is always best to be upfront with people rather than asking them to serve and then sharing with them in arrears your expectations. Set the standards and expectations upfront prior to inviting leadership commitments.

Leadership Covenant

Chapter 6 provides directions on creating a leadership covenant, which serves as a clarifying document that offers board members guidance on expectations and relational boundaries. While your board will probably be drafting a new covenant each year, the board's existing covenant may be a great tool for the nominations committee to identify future leaders and explain the expectations of board members.

An Invitation to Lead

Your members have been burned before. A pastor or a nominations committee member has called them, sharing that, "we need you on the _____ committee. No one else would say yes, so I need you to agree. Don't worry, it won't take up too much time. It's really just a committee on paper. There isn't any outside work to do, so all you will need to do is show up at the quarterly meetings." Well, we suppose some folks may jump at that incredibly compelling opportunity to serve Jesus, but perhaps a bit more thought and preparation is required! When we have low expectations of leaders, we will get low-quality investments from our leaders. While some faithful, gifted, and talented leaders may say "yes" to such an invitation, the committee will always be on their back-burners, and high-capacity leaders will instead channel their God-given talents to other pursuits they feel are valuable and where they can bring value.

With your change to an accountable and simplified leadership board, you have the opportunity to invite high-capacity leaders to REALLY make a meaningful impact both inside and outside the church. This won't be a committee on paper that meets a few times a year to write a report. Your board will be filled with agents of transformation, listening to the Holy Spirit, discerning God's vision, and guiding the congregation into the mission field in the name of Jesus Christ. So, make sure your invitation is personal by connecting the requirements and expectations for board members to the gifts you see in the invitee. Share last year's board covenant so the expectations are crystal clear.

Before prospective board members say "yes," they need to know that board service will require work: preparation before meetings, task assignments between meetings, difficult conversations about mission and accountability, the shouldering of risky ministry experiments, and bold leadership. Along the way, board members will learn, they will pray (A LOT), they will actually be able to make decisions instead of recommendations to yet another committee, they will receive encouragement and discover personal growth, and (most of all) they will have the opportunity to serve Jesus Christ, our Risen Savior, by steering the congregation toward a trajectory of reaching new people and disciple-making. Now, THAT's an invitation!

Checklist for Choosing the Team

- Ensure the Committee on Nominations and Leadership Development is fully aware of the needed spiritual gifts, leadership capacity, and "balcony" perspective required for Leadership Board service.
- Create and implement an intentional leadership development pathway.
- Create a compelling invitation to serve on the leadership board.
- Ensure prospective board members understand expectations before accepting a leadership role.

CHAPTER SIX

Getting Started

During the first year of simplified, accountable structure, it is a time to set new patterns, behaviors, rhythm, and methods of "doing business." We must hold ourselves accountable to one another to really do a new thing with this new structure. Otherwise, it will be the same old business in just a different configuration. Too often in my coaching, I (Kay) find congregations that simply conduct business as usual with fewer people or slip back into the old ruts without some intentionality of creating something new. Here are a few tips to consider for your first year in the new simplified, accountable structure:

- Practice accountability from the beginning.

- Do not be afraid to ask questions. Often others have the same questions, but do not ask them, either.

- Come with a sense of curiosity and grace.

- Have board members sit at the table and observers sit in chairs along the wall to clearly define those with voting responsibilities.

- After practicing for a couple of months, have your coach come and observe your meeting and help you course-correct as needed. It is difficult to stay on track with a new thing when you have not yet experienced it. It is a process you much live into. Repeat the process with your coach in a few more months.

- Configure your space to have meaningful conversation. Gather in a circle so you can see each other. Perhaps light a candle in the center representing Jesus at the table. I (Blake) once attended a church council meeting at a church I was coaching where all the board members were seated up front in a row and the "audience" were in rows in front of them. It reminded me of a City Council or School Board meeting where constituents could go up to the microphone to argue their point to the board. Meanwhile, the board members couldn't even see each other. The space and configuration dictated an "us/them" approach to everything that the board did.

- There are times when your board will need to take votes. Consensus is a fine enough goal, and it is great when the board is all in agreement, but consensus cannot be a requirement for your church to move forward. We have seen churches who utilize a unanimous consent require- ment become immobilized by a minority of members who control the church's future.

- Remember that guiding principles are living, breathing documents that are open to edits and additions as needed to provide permission-giving ministry within healthy boundaries.

- As you live into this new structure, your team may find edits or additions to the leadership covenant are in order.

In this chapter, we will explore the best practices of getting off the ground in the most effective and healthy way possible. Being intentional about the work ahead and focusing on the right stuff is absolutely critical. Before we begin the work in the new simplified, accountable structure we must first understand our roles clearly and how we function as a team with a new approach.

Four "Hats"

For members of the simplified structure to function in a healthy, faithful method, it is extremely important for the members and pastors to clearly understand how this new model works. In the traditional model, there were four committees (finance, trustees, staff-parish relations, and the council/board). Each committee met and operated separately within their specific area of responsibility. In this new model, there are NOT four separate meetings and areas of focus. Instead, the entire new board/council is jointly responsible for all four areas of responsibility. This inclusive responsibility creates a holistic approach. It is a comprehensive approach for leadership and allows for true governance. For example, rather than looking at an issue or decision through only the lens of finance, the board can widen the lens and approach the issue or decision through a holistic methodology considering the ramifications of finance, trustees, staff-parish, and the overall church.

Often in training for simplified structure, we ask attendees to imagine having four hats on the table in front of them. One hat is finance. The second is trustee. The third is staff-parish. The fourth is council. When the topic of finance is on the agenda, everyone picks up and wears their finance hat. Then, the finance hat comes off and the trustee hat comes on for a different part of the agenda pertaining to the facility. In other words, every person on the board has all responsibilities in all areas. To take the metaphor one step further, think of it another way. In the simplified structure, there are no longer four separate hats. There is now just one hat that covers all four areas of responsibility and authority: the single finance, trustee, SPR, council hat!

There will be times that work groups/teams from the board will be needed. Examples of the need for work groups might be to work on a preliminary budget to bring to the board for discussion and approval. Another example might be for a work group to work on some sort of policy manual and bring it back to the entire board for discussion and approval. A third example might be to put a work group together to work with the pastor on a proposed stewardship campaign to bring back to the board for discussion and approval. Do you see the theme here? They are work teams. Work teams do leg work, detail work, or preliminary work on behalf of the board. They work outside the larger board on some in-depth projects and then bring it back to the board for discussion and potential approval. Work teams do not have the authority to make decisions on their own. We have both worked with congregations in which the three SPR specialists completed the pastor's evaluation and submitted it to the district office without the knowledge or approval of the full board. Obviously, this is an unacceptable procedure.

Widen the circle for work groups. The board is not restricted to using only board members. People from the congregation with expertise or passion around certain topics or projects can be pulled into work groups. It is amazing the number of professionals that are sometimes in congregations that are never tapped to use their gifts and experiences in the life of the church. You may have folks from your congregation that would love to work on a short-term project but are not yet ready or able to be a leader. This is also a great time for potential leaders to engage at the next level as a growing opportunity.

Know your ROLE

Leadership Board Purpose

- The leadership board is accountable to Jesus Christ to guide the congregation in making disciples of Jesus Christ for the transformation of the world.

- Utilize a leadership style that combines accountability, responsibility, and authority

- Reduce micro management

- Synchronize and align all the church's ministries with the mission, vision, and goals

- Reduce the number of people engaged in administration and free up resources (time, gifts, talents, etc.) for hands-on ministry and engagement in the mission field

- Empower the pastor to lead

- Assist smaller congregations who cannot sustain the traditional structure

Leadership Board Responsibilities

- Confirm the vision cast by the pastor and establish annual and long-term goals for the church

- Work in partnership with programs and ministries to ensure ministries and teams all fulfill the mission and vision of the church

- Establish the church's yearly budget

- Work with the District Superintendent to hold the pastor accountable

Pastor's Role

- Cast the church's vision

- Hire, supervise, assess (and if needed, terminate) both paid and unpaid staff

- Hold staff (paid and unpaid) accountable for leading their ministry areas and fulfilling the mission and vision of the church

- Monitor the accomplishment of church goals and make adjustments as required to ensure achievement of those goals

Meeting Attendance

The *BOD* requires all board meetings to be open meetings. The primary exception is when the board goes into executive session so that S/PPR issues can be discussed. Since meetings are open, it will be important to set up the room to help people learn the model more effectively. A best practice is for board members to gather around a table and other attendees to sit around the room perimeter. This clearly denotes who is eligible to vote and who is not. It also allows for better control of the agenda.

Staff may be eligible to attend, but are not required. In fact, we suggest staff not attend. Remember, the pastor is accountable to the board, not staff. The staff is accountable to the pastor. When staff is present at board meetings, they get sucked into conversations. Accountability is more difficult and management conversations are more likely to creep into the agenda. An exception to the "no staff" suggestion might be executive pastors with significant leadership roles at very large churches.

In our experience, once the board gets up and running, the attendance from those other than the board is rare. There seems to be an inverse relationship between trust in the leadership and attendance in the open sessions of the board meeting. When accountable leadership is modeled, the trust of the congregation is built and people are comfortable engaging in ministry teams (the most important work) rather than church administration. If several people are showing up to observe the board meetings, you probably need to be rethinking your communications and transparency.

Leadership Covenant

When the new board gathers each year for the first time,

covenant together. A covenant is a sacred agreement with God and other board members. This covenant is a written agreement of the expectations and a code of conduct for which each board member agrees upon. Without a covenant, there will most likely be ambiguity. A healthy team covenants together and expectations are known and agreed upon before the work begins. In Kay's consulting, she would always suggest the covenant starts from scratch each year. The previous board would not want to impose last year's covenant on the current board. Of course, it can be used as a template, but copying last year's over to this year takes away from its sacredness, the opportunity for new people to weigh in on its content, and the exercise of a fresh start and perspective each year. Once the covenant is agreed upon and put into writing, have each board member sign the covenant. This is a sacred time and practice, so approach it appropriately.

I (Kay) am often asked for a copy of a leadership covenant. I hesitate to offer one as I see too many times that churches will not go through the process and discernment to create one their church leaders "own" and therefore was not imposed onto them. However, in the spirit of being a resource to get you started, please consider the following as possible inclusions of your leadership covenant:

Sample Leadership Covenant

- Board members are encouraged to invest in conversations and decisions with vigor and passion. However, once the board has come to a decision, each board member will openly and publicly support the decision of the board whether the individual member personally agrees with the decision. We are a board with a unified voice.

- Board members are expected to be present at all board

meetings unless ill or out of town. If members miss more than three meetings, the board chair will converse with the board member to see if their seat needs to be vacated and filled by someone who can be more active.

- Board members will review the meeting packet prior to meeting, coming fully prepared and ready to participate.

- Board members are role models for the congregation. Therefore, members will model mature discipleship by being present in worship at least three times per month, tithing or moving toward a tithe, have an active prayer life, serve in mission three times per year, be active in a ministry team, be in a faith development group, and openly share their faith with others in the secular world.

- Board members will be on time for meetings, silence cell phones, and immerse themselves in the meeting without distractions in respect for others' time and commitment.

- Board members will encourage and support our pastors and fellow board members.

- Board members will hold ourselves, the pastors, and other board members accountable for their leadership roles and responsibilities. This includes allowing others to hold the board members collectively and individually accountable.

- Board Members understand that conflict and disagreements are natural in any community, including the church. As a board, we will approach matters of disagreement with transparency and maintain our missional focus as a board. When approached by a person or group concerning a matter of disagreement or conflict, we will follow the path laid out by Jesus on Matthew 18 by encouraging the concerned party to go directly to the individual, to volunteer to go with the concerned party as a witness, or to invite the concerned party to address the full leadership or an assigned work team to address the issue. At no time will we support secret meetings that undermine the integrity or authority of the pastor or Board.

Add other covenantal elements that define the roles and authority of each board member individually and collectively, such as boundaries about making demands upon staff and staff time without consulting the pastor, matters of conflicts of interest, and the limits of personal authority as a board member.

Guiding Principles

Guiding principles are a set of policies and procedures which allow the ministry of the church to function on a day-to-day basis within healthy boundaries. Guiding principles keep the board from managing and the pastor and/or staff from micro-managing. These principles are permission-giving strategies that protect the overall health and well-being of the church.

Most churches start with a blank piece of paper in creating their guiding principles. While all of us have our United Methodist Church's *Book of Discipline (BOD)* to guide and direct us, there is certainly a need for local policies and procedures. Guiding principles compliment the *BOD*. They might also further clarify the *BOD* in the local context.

Think of the guiding principles as a living, breathing document. Because our environment (people, ministries, community, etc.) changes constantly, guiding principles will need to grow and adapt themselves as needed. Some churches might have some existing policies or procedures that might be adopted or adapted for the guiding principles.

A church might also refer to policies and procedures (i.e. employee manual) in the guiding principles as a reference to their acceptance or knowledge.

Allow us to offer a filter challenge. Every time a decision is made by the board, ask yourself if there could be a guiding principle established or modified that would have allowed the decision to be made earlier and/or without the board's intervention. Please hear us. We are not suggesting that a guiding principle be needed for everything. Yet, many times, we could allow for more natural and timely flow if the board could grant permission within guidelines through a guiding principle. Here are some topics to consider as you write your guiding principles. Keep in mind that this is not an exhaustive list, but rather one to help you begin to consider what guiding principles are needed for your church.

Potential Topics for Guiding Principle Consideration

- Mission, vision, core values of the church
- Identification the board's role, powers, responsibilities, and authority, in regards to the *Book of Discipline*
- Financial approval rules for staff, the pastor, and the building maintenance team
- Hiring/terminating authority of the pastor and other paid staff
- References to church wide policies:
  o Building and equipment usage policies (for example, rental policies for members, internal ministry groups, outside non-profit groups or for-profit businesses)
  o Safe sanctuary policies for child protection
  o Employee handbook

- o Building safety

- o Internet usage

- Parliamentary rules of order, such as the usage of Roberts Rules of Order, the consensus method, or other variations

- Include how to change a guiding principle

- Official record keeping and access to records of meetings and executive session minutes

- Role and function of the building maintenance team

- Authority and responsibility of the treasurer

- Relationship of Nominations and Lay Leadership Development to the Leadership board

- Boundaries that state how individual board members may make (or not) demands on staff time outside formal board requests

- How daycare and/or preschool relate to the church, pastor, and leadership board (There is a huge legal and governance difference between childcare ministries that operate under a church's ministry and childcare ministries that exist as a separate but related 501(c)(3). These differences will impact how your write your guiding principle defining the relationship.)

- Defining public meetings vs executive session (such as personnel matters when the board is operating as the congregation's S/PPRC).

Just like with the leadership covenant, I (Kay) am often asked for a sample of guiding principles. Again, I hesitate to offer a sample because so many will just adopt the sample and be done. If this were done, the whole spirit and purpose of the exercise is missed. It also does not address the intention of this being a fluid document that easily and frequently shifts as needed. However, once again in the spirit of trying to offer resources, we offer the following as samples of some possible guiding principles. Note that some of these items conflict with one another. It is up to your transition team and the Charge Conference to discern how you wish to balance the responsibilities and authority of the board and pastor.

Sample Guiding Principles

- All references to the Church Council, Board of Trustees, Staff/Pastor Parish Relations Committee, Endowment Committee, and Finance Committee, in all congregational policies as of _____, and in all references in the *Book of Discipline of the United Methodist Church*, shall be understood to refer to the Leadership Team beginning _____.

- Once the budget is approved, those responsible (i.e. staff and team leaders) for the various ministry areas have the authority to spend their budget to align with the objectives for their ministry area approved by the pastor. No further approval is needed to access the budget in their area of responsibility. *

- The pastor is responsible for reviewing line items within ministry areas with staff and team leaders for accountability from the staff and to the board.

- Any member of the Building Maintenance Team has the authority to purchase supplies for building mainte- nance and improvement up to $_____ without approval. The Building Maintenance Team leader can authorize purchases for building maintenance and improvement up to $_____. Purchases up to $_____ can be approved by the pastor. Any purchases over $_____ need Leadership Board approval unless the expenditure is already approved in a capital expenditure line item in the approved budget. *

- Any expenditure over $_____ will require three bids. Preference will be given to hire local companies offering competitive bids within 5 percent of other bids. If the expenditure is already approved in the budget and meets the previous criteria, there is no further approval needed.*

- The pastor has the authority to hire and release employees using the church's employee policies. When terminating an employee, the pastor will invite a board member to sit in.

- The authority to hire and terminate employees of the church shall be vested in the Leadership Board. The pastor shall have the authority to interview and recommend candidates to fill open staff positions. The Board shall have the sole authority to determine the number of staff positions, approve job descriptions for each staff member and set the salary paid to each staff member. The Leadership Board delegates to the pastor the authority to supervise, discipline, and manage paid staff.

- The pastor will review all paid staff annually using the approval evaluation process in the employee manual dated _____. Paid staff will review unpaid staff/team and leaders annually using the same evaluation process.

---

* The treasurer must be consulted concerning any single purchase or expenditure over $_____ for purposes of cash flow. The treasurer does not approve or deny purchases but rather confirms large purchases will not create cash flow issues.

- The Weekday Child Care Advisory Board (*BOD* Paragraph 256.2.c) is fully amenable and accountable to the Leadership Board, and shall submit an annual budget and recommended policy changes to the Leadership Board. Financial reports will be submitted to the Board monthly. The director of weekday ministries is supervised by the pastor.

- The board recognizes and approves the Building Usage Policies dated _____.

- The board recognizes and approves the Building Security and Key Policies dated _____.

- The board recognizes and approves the Financial Controls Policies dated _____.

- All meetings of the Leadership Board shall be open to the public, with the exception of any meeting or portion of a meeting in which a personnel matter or a matter of legal negotiations is considered. In those cases, the Board will go into executive session. Minutes of executive session agenda items concerning personnel matters will be kept separately as part of the S/PPRC files.

- Leadership Board members are nominated by a separate and independent Nominating Committee, chaired by the pastor, and elected by the Charge Conference as described in the *BOD*. Due to Leadership Board's serving as the congregation's Staff-Parish Relations Committee, no immediate family member of the pastor or other paid staff person may serve as a member of the board. Due to serving as the congregation's Board of Trustees, only Leadership Board members over the age eighteen will have voting privileges in matters of property, incorporation, legal matters, contracts, insurance, investments, or other matters described in the *BOD* paragraphs 2525-2551.

At your first meeting:

- Create and join in a Leadership Covenant. A covenant is a sacred agreement with God and other board members. This covenant is a written agreement of the expectations and a code of conduct which should be agreed upon by the entire board. Without a covenant, there will most likely be ambiguity.

- Explain and discuss your model agenda for healthy board meetings (See Chapter 8).

- Elect a Chair of Trustees (annual requirement) from the Board's membership. We recommend that the Leadership Board Chair be elected by the Board to also serve as trustee chair.

- Spend quality time working on the Guiding Principles. It will pay dividends for years to come! Be sure to orient the Board on Guiding Principles every year.

- Share and discuss the Accountable Leadership Cycle (See Chapter 3).

- Schedule the board meetings for the year (See Chapter 10 for an outline of work for a whole year of monthly meetings).

CHAPTER SEVEN

Adaptive Leadership:
Changing the Conversation at the Table

You have your structure set. Guiding principles are published. A leadership covenant has been created and signed. Now it's time to have a meeting, right? But wait! Don't fall into the trap of thinking a new structure will automatically create better conversations at the table. Now is the time to deeply consider how adaptive leadership changes the very nature of leadership.

The biblical narrative of the Jerusalem Council in Acts 15 shows us an example of ancient adaptive leadership. The fledgling church had to consider a new way of being (the potential inclusion of Gentiles into the church) while staying connected to their traditions and identity. There was deep disagreement, and because the matter was important, the disagreement was deeply felt. The leaders looked at the mission of the church as defined in the Great Commission and the Great Commandment of Love and figured out a pathway into an unknown future. The decision was then communicated to the larger church through representatives and an apostolic letter.

When teaching a course of study class on polity and administration, I (Blake) was assisting a new pastor in understanding the principles of the simplified structure model, and, of course, the concepts of accountable and adaptive leadership came up. His assignment: write up a process to manage the divergent paths that members wanted to take in leadership. As we dug deeper, the matter of Robert's Rules of Order came up again and again. Apparently, the congregation had learned along the way that correct parliamentary procedure was the answer to their problems. The difficulty now was that "doing business right" was unable to solve the complex problems the church was facing. The concern couldn't be fixed by a technical change of better parliamentary processes of motions and seconds. So, we decided on a radical course of action: an entire season of talking about ministry: of discernment, of discovery, and of conversation … with no motions and no voting allowed.

Instead of everything in good order, and each "side" trying to "win" by having enough votes, the board would focus on being prayerfully dedicated to Christ's mission and vision for the congregation, and it would experiment with different processes to come to decisions. We are living in a complex culture very different than the one in which our churches were founded.

The solutions which worked so well for us in the past are now anchors pulling us underwater. There is a popular saying in the business world: "what got us here won't get us there." Technical changes are not enough to get us into Christ's God-sized dream for your congregation. The technical changes of restructure (simplification) and accountable leadership provide space and a place for adaptive leadership (missional creativity).

There have been many books written about adaptive leadership, both secular and church-related. Tod Bolsinger has gifted the church with an excellent metaphor of "canoeing the mountains" by comparing adaptive leadership to the explorations of Lewis and Clark as they literally created the map of the west for the young U.S. government. They had expected to find a river that would flow all the way to the Pacific Ocean, but instead they had to figure a way to turn their canoeing skills into mountaineering skills when they ran into the Rockies (see Bolsinger's *Canoeing the Mountains: Christian Leadership in Uncharted Territory*).

As part of his consultation work with the Arkansas Conference, Alban Institute Consultant Gil Rendle used a story about taking one step at a time to help our entire conference re-imagine leadership and ministry for a new generation. Gil asked us to imagine a mother sending her son to lock up the barn doors at night. It was dark, and the son couldn't see the barn, much less the doors. So, his mother gives him a flashlight and sends him out again. The son comes back. The flashlight, while appreciated, still is too dim to help him find the barn. The mother sends him out a third time, saying, "you don't need to see the barn. You know the basic direction. Just keep walking to the end of the light."

As the son walks forward the path was illuminated more with every step. Eventually, the barn, was revealed. All he needed was a little faith that the barn was in a certain direction, the flashlight as a tool to help him move forward, and a willingness to take each step. (Gil, now retired from the Texas Methodist Foundation, later published this story in *Doing the Math of Mission: Fruits, Faithfulness, and Metrics*). In rural Arkansas, this story had quite a resonance. Many of our lay and clergy annual conference members had grown up on or still lived on farms. They knew the darkness of night outside the city limits. These metaphors and stories helped us see that part of adaptive leadership meant that we needed some level of comfort with the unknown and the uncharted. We could set some proximate goals, be clear about our direction, and start heading toward making an impact for Christ. We didn't need to know and plan for every step, and, in fact, we *couldn't* know every step of the journey. Our world and the soul of every person are simply too complex. We would have to monitor and adjust. We would have to be willing to **adapt**.

The legacy forms of leadership and structure we have inherited are simply not built to adapt. These legacy forms of structure and the style of leadership they encourage are about fixing problems to get the church "back to business." Business, in this case, usually means back to focusing on membership (not discipleship or evangelism) and making folks feel comfortable (rather than transforming the world). The multiple committees and "checks and balances" built into our inherited structures are all about maintaining the *status quo*. But the *status* ain't *quo*. The church is losing ground, and lives aren't being transformed. Disciples aren't being made.

Your church needs to be able to adapt to uncharted territory, like setting proximate goals, being brutally clear about the mission and vision you have discerned, and holding one another accountable to making an impact for Christ. By placing these adaptive leadership responsibilities into your single board, you are enabling your church to get out of a maintenance mode and into transformation mode.

Those churches that truly grow into a new structure with accountable and adaptive leadership have experienced a positive change in the trajectory of their church. The changes do not occur overnight. The changes are not easy nor do they come naturally. But for those churches that are truly committed to leading a church on its mission and are willing to make the shifts necessary to do so, the outcomes are remarkable. First, there is a renewed healthiness in the leaders. Second, there is a change in the nature and content of conversation around the leadership table. Third, hope is reborn within the life of the congregation. Fourth, there is a deepened commitment and understanding of the mission of making disciples. Fifth, a missional focus unifies the congregation since someone is piloting the ship. All the passengers know the itinerary. All the passengers realize they are on a working ship (like an aircraft carrier on a mission and not a cruise ship being entertained) and know their assigned task as part of the team. Sixth, there is the opportunity to create shared, common language -- first within the board and continuing as the board guides the larger congregation into uncharted waters.

Time for Adaptive Change

As the board makes the technical changes of consolidating the four administrative teams, the opportunity for adaptive changes are now upon them. The technical change of having the people representing the collective functions of trustees, finance, council, and SPR in the room at the same time is something we could imagine. This was most likely one of the motivating factors to move into this simplified structure. Now is the time the adaptive changes will need to kick into gear. Remember, adaptive change is all about implementing changes we do not necessarily know how to implement. Be patient with yourself and one another, but hold each other accountable for living into the adaptive changes. The two biggest shifts for adaptive change are the change in agenda, conversation, and focus. The board is to govern, not manage, the day to day operations of the church. To adequately govern, the board must take a balcony view. Most churches find it difficult to move from the typical ground view (management) to the balcony view (governance). They historically have just not functioned at that level.

If the board changes the agenda as recommended, it will allow for this adaptive shift to begin. If the new simplified board uses the old agenda, the board will typically only make the technical change of having fewer people around the table, but not change the conversation at the table. Adaptive changes take shifts in our values, beliefs, attitudes, and/or behaviors. As you can imagine, these types of changes are much more difficult to implement than changing the number of people on a nominations report or the number of meetings scheduled!

Remember, technical changes are about solving known problems with known solutions. Adaptive changes result from addressing complex problems with creative solutions. Adaptive change starts with adaptive thinking and adaptive learning. We must be willing to take on new thoughts, understandings, and behaviors in order to achieve adaptive changes.

Adaptive leadership means risk, both from external factors (experiments sometimes fail) and internal factors, particularly sabotage from members concerned about all the changes happening. The more your board focuses your congregation on the disciple-making mission, the more others with peripheral concerns or feelings of lost power will criticize the direction. I (Blake) remember from Latin class that the word "decide" means "to cut off." As your board makes decisions, folks will feel cut off or cut out.

Gil Rendle writes about this experience in his book, *Next Steps in the Wilderness (pages 8-9):*

> *"Adaptive work is not tidy. In his theory of change from a systems perspective that takes into consideration the insights of chaos theory, organizational consultant John Scherer notes that in order*

for change to be birthed, two "parents" must be present— pain and possibility. There must be a discomfort sufficiently strong to make the people want to be different and a possibility promising enough to support the people through change. Walter Brueggemann once commented that the central task of leadership is to manage the hopes and the fears of the people. Indeed, managing hopes and fears—pain and possibility—in a congregation, a conference, or a corporation is a spiritual task of great faithfulness. Scherer demonstrates that if the leader can surface the appropriate pain, hold clearly the possibility of what can be, and help people let go of old assumptions, then the people will enter a stage of chaos—the truly creative environment where change happens.

It may be helpful to recall that the wilderness is required. In Mark's gospel, as soon as John baptized Jesus in the Jordan and the voice from heaven proclaimed Jesus as God's son, we are told that the Spirit immediately drove Jesus into the wilderness (Mark 1:12). Wilderness, chaos, change is neither tidy nor comfortable, which underscores the true difficulty of adaptive leadership in a system designed for the comfort of problem-solving management."

The wilderness is a difficult place. Like the explorations of Lewis and Clark, it is often uncharted, and like the story of the boy finding the barn, it can feel incredibly dark out there with your meager flashlight. Your board's job is to keep pointing toward the "Promised Land of God" while carefully and prayerfully dealing with the inevitable push back and sabotage inherent with adaptive leadership. Moses had to deal with the "Back to Egypt Committee" of murmurers (Exodus 16) who were more comfortable with slavery than the unknown. Your board will need to help each other, and the larger congregation, stay on track with the larger mission and vision that you have discerned. Keep casting the vision. Vision leaks!

Staying on Track

Part of adaptive change is holding your fellow board members accountable to not only the Leadership Covenant, but also to the role of governance. If one of your fellow board members ventures out into what we refer to as the "tall grass" of management, it is your responsibility to call the member into accountability of their governance role. Of course, we do this with love and grace! But we must do it. If we do not, we will soon find ourselves returning to our comfortable management tendencies where once again no one is steering the missional ship!

Some churches we have worked with have had some real fun with helping everyone stay in the governing mode. Some have developed some pretty creative strategies, too. Some use vocal reminders such as "tall grass," "time out," or "management warning" to reign back in the conversation. Other churches have developed hand signals such as a time-out symbol or putting their hand up in the well-known stop signal. Others have placed an object in the middle of the table to be picked up when the conversation has veered off track. Use a method that fits your board's personality and context. The method might even change from time to time. The important part is to have some sort of method to help a person recognize their drifting and get things back on track quickly, efficiently, and without debilitating the team.

God-sized Goals

In Chapter 3, we shared about how setting goals and measuring fruitfulness is the basis of accountable leadership. Adaptive leadership is about making sure that the goals we set are actually creative and compelling God-sized goals and not merely quick fixes. We must also be sure that goals set are not just for the sake of setting goals, but are the next intentional steps in living into God's preferred future - the discerned vision. Alignment to the mission (making disciples) and the vision (God's preferred future for the unique way your church makes disciples) is essential.

Alignment

It is the responsibility of the board, pastor, and staff to ensure alignment at all levels. There are three key areas of alignment: budget, calendar, and staff. It is the responsibility of the board to ensure the budget aligns with the mission, vision, goals, and core values. For example, we would be kidding ourselves to say that we value children if we have no children's ministry budget or this is the first place we cut funding. Too many times the budget drives the church. Allow the mission to drive the budget. The budget should be a result of the needs identified to create the objectives to accomplish the goals.

The calendar indicates what we value and how we use our time and energy. The calendar is a result of the objectives derived from the goals, vision, mission, and core values. The calendar should reflect ministries and activities that align to our stated goals. If we simply copy our calendar over from one year to the next, we are a calendar-driven rather than a mission-driven church. The pastor is accountable for the calendar alignment with the staff.

Paid staffing should typically be fifty percent of a stable church's budget. For a growing church or a church in a more metropolitan area, the percentage might be as high as sixty percent. Typically, when the paid staff budget is out of whack, we see congregations hiring staff to do the ministry rather than equipping the congregation to do the ministry. Staff (whether it is paid staff or volunteer staff) need to be aligned with the goals and specifically the objectives of their ministry area. We must ensure our staff is spending their time, energy, and budget on the areas the board has deemed the focus (mission, vision, goals).

The most detrimental kind of staff to keep on the payroll are staff that we hire out of charity. Feeling sorry for someone is understandable and it is great to offer to help folks. But that help needs to come out of the mission fund, not the personnel budget. Low performing staff will drag down your church's mission to their comfort level.

Strategic Planning and a Simplified Accountable Leadership Board

Strategic planning is a part of what it means to serve as accountable and adaptive leaders. It is about claiming that balcony space.

In addition to monthly checks on progress on your God-sized goals and impact in your congregation's mission field, your leadership team should take a strategic planning retreat annually so that you can spend adequate time together discerning your congregation's future. We share more about the annual retreat in Chapter 10, which also outlines an entire year in leadership.

In Kay's book, *Gear Up: Nine Essential Processes for the Optimized Church,* she goes into detail on strategic ministry planning (one of her favorite topics). Also, you can refer to her workbook, *Strategic Ministry Planning Workbook,* which she wrote with some partners. You will find the Kindle e-book on Amazon. Allow us to provide a quick overview of the five parts of strategic ministry planning.

Mission: The purpose for the church – why you exist. Every church exists to make disciples of Jesus Christ for the transformation of the world as Matthew 28:19-20 indicates. It also happens to be the mission statement of the United Methodist Church as indicated in paragraph 120 of the *BOD:*

¶ **120.** *The Mission—The mission of the Church is to make disciples of Jesus Christ for the transformation of the world. Local churches and extension ministries of the Church provide the most significant arenas through which disciple-making occurs.*

Please do not waste any more time trying to figure out the mission of your church. It has been clearly laid out for us. Embrace it! The board is accountable to Jesus Christ for the church being faithful in making disciples for the transformation of the world.

Vision: A church's vision connects its purpose, its identity, and its narrative. This is the unique method that your church uses to make disciples in your local context. Vision is your preferred future. Vision emerges from the sweet spot of the gifts of your congregation, the passions of your leaders, and the needs of your community. In today's quick paced culture, vision usually needs to be re-cast every couple of years. The pastor is accountable for articulating the congregation's vision. Lovett Weems, the retired director of the Lewis Center for Church Leadership at Wesley Theological Seminary, shared in his book, *Church Leadership* (p. 96), that a key question for leaders is, "Are you willing to wear the vision the same way that people wear clothes?" Vision provides the energy, momentum, and enthusiasm for church vitality.

Core Values: Values exist in your church whether you have named them or not. Think of it as your DNA. It is who you are. They guide your decisions. Core values are usually fairly static unless there is intentionality in moving towards aspirational values. Even if there is intentionality in moving towards aspirational values, this shift is normally slow. If you have not identified your core values, now is the time to do it. There is a worksheet to get your started in the strategic planning workbook mentioned above.

Beware of fully aspirational values because they can't be a foundation for realistic plans. Bishop Gary Mueller of Arkansas often warns our cabinet not to create plans "strapped to the backs of unicorns."

God-sized Goals: These are the action steps to be taken in the upcoming year that will allow you to live into your vision and mission. Usually there are three to five big over-all God-sized goals named each year to focus your congregation's resources. Some of your goals may be multi-year goals that need to updating based on your experiencing of the last year. The board holds the pastor accountable for goals and casting/articulating the vision.

Objectives: This is where the rubber hits the road. Objectives are where the goals grow hands and feet. The staff (paid and unpaid – aka ministry team leaders) are responsible for the creating and implementing the objectives to make an impact in fulfilling the congregation's goals. In the account-able leadership model, the pastor holds the staff and/or ministry team leaders responsible for meeting the objectives.

CHECKLIST FOR ADAPTIVE LEADERSHIP

- Ensure there is alignment: calendar, budget, and staff
- Hold one another accountable to adaptive leadership and governance rather than technical changes and management
- Conduct annual strategic planning retreat
- Ensure regular accountability to the goals set at the strategic planning retreat
- Be willing to walk in the wilderness as you grow and live into your understanding and practice of adaptive leadership.

CHAPTER EIGHT

Board Meetings
that Make a Difference

When I was serving as a local church pastor, I (Blake) had the joy of serving alongside some excellent lay leaders in congregations, and while we certainly took our mission seriously, we tried to carry our responsibility with a bit of fun. After a series of multiple back-to-back meetings, one of my mischievous lay leaders presented me with a blue "participation award" ribbon emblazoned with an image of a coffee mug and a statement of deep and abiding truth written in gold foil. The ribbon said, "I survived another meeting that should have been an email."

When the purpose of a meeting is misunderstood, preparatory work is inadequate, or the agenda is disorganized, you and your fellow leaders will miss a leadership opportunity. Bad meetings create a lack of ownership in the group's process and actions, encourages apathy, and degrades your leadership capacity as a team.

Changing the number of people around the table is never enough. You also will need to change the conversation at the table. If you move toward a simplified accountable leadership structure, but continue to use the legacy Robert's Rules of Order agenda (old business, then new business, and filled with endless oral reports), your new board will never be able to operate in a new way. It is time to create an agenda that reflects your goals, uses time efficiently, and assumes personal accountability of board members to come prepared to lead.

"Consent Calendar Items" and The Packet

At least a week prior to the leadership council meeting, a packet of documents will be emailed to each leadership team member for review prior to the meeting. This prepares the leaders for what Roberts' Rules of Order calls the consent calendar section of the agenda. Sending the packet out ahead of time keeps the team from having to take time during the meeting to read reports or listen to long (and often unprepared) oral reports. This also allows plenty of time to fully review the information and be prepared with questions, comments, or concerns as well as the ability to fully participate in conversations and decisions. For instance, the minutes of the previous meeting need only to be edited or approved since the leadership covenants to review the minutes before arrival. The financial report needs no approval unless there are changes to the budget that was already approved. A single covering motion can take care of any "approval" items in the packet, including the minutes. If something needs to be removed from the consent items, you can do that and shift the item later in the agenda.

Preferably, the packet will be prepared by a person in a church administrative position (i.e. operations manager, church secretary) and reviewed by the board chair and pastor before it is distributed. Likely, the administrative person will need to send out reminders to people contributing to the packet. The pastor will hold the administrative person accountable for its timeliness, accuracy, and thoroughness.

The packet's purpose is to provide information for board

members to keep them abreast of the current status of the church as well as receive information ahead of the meeting giving each member the time to review. The packet is provided as both a resource for communication and a tool of preparation. Members of the leadership team should have read the packet and come prepared to either vote approval for the items or to move the items toward the discussion phase of the agenda.

Below is a list of the recommended contents for the board meeting packet:

❑ **Agenda**   See the agenda section in this chapter for more information.

❑ **Covenant**   The signed Leadership Covenant is an ongoing reminder.

❑ **Vital Signs** Vital signs provide a dashboard of the latest information, metrics, and trends that are extremely important for leaders to know and understand. Vital signs include: worship attendance, professions of faith, small group participation, missional participation, and financial giving. The church is already tracking this information and sent it to the general church for tracking and statistics. To start, the board may need to see the past five years' trends if this is new information to the members. Subsequently, the year's trends and how they compare to the previous year is probably adequate. All this information can be obtained from your conference dashboard or your district office.

❏ **Describe-ables** Not all fruits of ministry will show up in the metrics of the vital signs mentioned above. Those fruits are what we refer to as the describe-ables or the stories of vital ministries. What lives are being touched by the ministries of the church? How are people growing in their faith? How is the church impacting the community in the name of Christ? The pastor will provide any pertinent describe-ables in the packet for the board.

❏ **Guests** This may be new information to capture. Record the number of first-time guests the church hosts each week. Also, record the number of second-time guests each week. These are important numbers to know and track. While numbers do not tell us the whole story, they are indeed early indicators. These two particular numbers help us catch a glimpse of how well three of our systems are working: evangelism, hospitality, and connection. (See *Gear Up* or *IMPACT!* for more information on these systems.) If we are not having first-time guests, we know the church is struggling with evangelism. If the church is having first-time guests, but not returning guests, we know we likely have either a hospitality and/or connection issue which needs to be addressed.

❏ **Minutes** Minutes of the previous board meeting as submitted by the acting recording secretary.

❑ **Financials** These reports should include a budget vs actual report for each category (not each line item) and a comprehensive balance sheet. There may be a note attached from the treasurer if there is something out of the ordinary or noteworthy for the board to know or understand. For example, some board members might panic at the "summer slump" generosity numbers. The treasurer might include an income statement from the previous year showing the trend is to be expected and the church is on track to match or exceed last year's giving numbers.

❑ **Goals** The pastor will provide a written update on progress on congregational goals and outline any strategy-level decisions that she may need from the board to move forward on the goals.

❑ **Reports** While we do not suggest requiring the inclusion of a stack of monthly ministry team reports, there may be a group that just feels strongly compelled to share information with the board. A group can write a report to include in the packet with the permission of the chair. If a church must have reports, one suggestion is to have a standard report form with some simple questions that clearly asks at the beginning if the special report is an update or if some sort of council/board action is required. This may keep reporting ministry teams on mission and clear about why they are reporting. In one church I served, I (Blake) created a simple standardized reporting form that was available online. One of the first questions, after the contact information, required the reporting individual or group to click a box indicating whether the report required action on the part of the church council or if it was "for information only." It also required submitters of proposals to describe any financial implications. See a sample reporting form in Appendix G.

❏ **Specials** From time to time, there may be special reports, information, bids, etc. which need to be shared with the board. For example, there may be roof bids included for a planned capital expenditure. If the board is working on a new policy, a board member might include some preliminary work towards the project as a springboard of the work of the entire board. For the pastor's evaluation to be submitted to the district superintendent, there may be information or a worksheet inserted into the packet.

The Agenda

The agenda is a guide for the most effective and efficient use of time and resources of the board members. It is a plan of action. Working the plan allows us to be good stewards of our time and resources. Agendas are crucial and a necessary tool for effective, efficient leadership. Without an agenda, conversations will drift off topic and we might not tend to the top priorities.

In the beginning, the board may not be as efficient as they will become over time as they practice the model. You will most likely come to a point where the board can finish their meeting in about ninety minutes. Of course, there will be times when longer meetings are needed, but most will be able to work within the ninety-minute format. The agenda is comprised of three major portions that could be chunked in about thirty-minute segments. Spend one-third of your time in spiritual and leadership development. Spend one-third of your time on goal and people evaluation. Spend the remaining one-third of your time on problem solving and generative work.

We suggest creating a "docket" format that includes a running time for each agenda item, so that the board members can appropriately budget their discussion time. Estimating a realistic amount of time for each item requires some preparation work. If you have a dozen members on your board, but only schedule five minutes for the discussion of an item, then you are expecting everyone to have well under thirty seconds to speak, and that does not include the time taken to vote or come to consensus on an issue.

In preparing the agenda, the board chair can send a notice out to board members asking if there are any items that might need to be discussed. We say "might" because not every item requested needs to be on a board agenda. Some matters need to be held off-line or by a task force or other group before it is ripe for inclusion in the board's agenda, and some items are simply not the work of the board. If the matter is to be properly vetted before the board, then the board chair should do some organizational preparation. First, get clarity of the purpose of an item (is it about making a decision, answering a question, or simply sharing information?). Second, estimate the time required. Third, prepare a proposed process for addressing the matter (such as taking a few minutes a discussion followed by a vote or suggesting a new guiding principle to handle similar matters in the future).

You will want to meet monthly in the beginning. In a year or two, you might be able to move to bi-monthly meetings, but less meetings is never the goal. Fulfillment of Jesus' mission always comes first. Kay has worked with churches that have used the simplified accountable structure for years and have quarterly meetings. But in the beginning, while setting up policies, procedures, and Guiding Principles, the board will likely need to meet monthly. Note that even if your board has created a tradition of less frequent meetings, when you receive a new pastor, the board will need to switch back to monthly (or even more frequent) meetings.

On each and every agenda for the board (including all other church agendas), print the mission (making disciples...), vision, and core values of the church. This is a great reminder of the basis and focus of our conversations and decisions. One church Kay worked with had large posters printed with their mission, vision, and core values and posted them in the room where the board normally met. Not only was this a great reminder for the board members, but every person who used that same room were also reminded.

In this chapter you will find a sample agenda and an annotated explanation of each agenda item. This basic format can be used for each meeting, with the understanding that some meetings, such as the annual pastoral assessment, may require adjustments in the schedule and flow of the agenda. Notice the order of the agenda. It might appear as though the agenda is reversed and familiar items are missing from your typical board agenda. This is very intentional. The items of most importance are at the top. If the first few items were placed as additions to the bottom of the agenda, we would never have time for those items! Also, notice there are no oral reports from committees on this agenda. This is certainly intentional and not an oversight. The purpose of the board is not to hear reports.

The purpose of the board is to govern, guide, and set policies by being the congregation's lead body for generative, fiduciary, and strategic work. The day-to-day ministries which make up the activities of the church should always reflect the congregational goals articulated by the board. Those objectives established by staff to relate to the goals all roll up into the goal report from the pastor. If the board spends time hearing about each and every ministry, they are in management mode at ground level.

The job of the board is to be in the balcony with a missional focus, overseeing the entire "dance floor" of vital ministry and the congregation's relationship with the community. When I (Blake) served as an executive pastor in a large multi-staff congregation, I would often attempt to explain staff responsibilities in comparison to a naval ship's executive officer. I, as the executive pastor, was in charge of the ship and the senior pastor was the captain responsible for the ocean. Adapting this staffing metaphor to the leadership of a governing board, the simplified, accountable leadership board is responsible for the ocean --- the direction and mission of the "ship" of the church and its impact on individual lives, neighborhoods, and communities, and the larger world. Your agenda needs to reflect this larger role and tremendous responsibility.

Sample Agenda for Simplified Accountable Leadership

On the following page, you will find a sample agenda for your review. On the next page, you will find an explanation of each agenda item.

First United Methodist Church
Leadership Team Meeting
Date_____

*Our Mission: To make new disciples of Jesus Christ
for the transformation of the world.*

*Our Vision: Each of us at FUMC is on a journey to grow closer
to God, to be more like Jesus, and to be filled with the Holy Spirit. No
matter where you are in your walk with Christ, you are
invited to journey and grow with us, through the power of
the Holy Spirit, so that we can fulfill God's commission.*

*Core Values: Excellence, evangelism, engagement,
equipping, expansion, and encouragement.*

6:00pm	Opening Prayer	Jennifer Jackson, Chair
6:00pm	Spiritual Formation	David Dent
6:15pm	Leadership Equipping	Carol Clark
6:30pm	Review of New People	Pastor Taylor
6:35pm	Goal Review and	
	Accountability Conversation	Pastor Taylor
6:50pm	Packet and Consent Calendar Items	
6:55pm	Generative and Strategic Work	Jennifer Jackson
	6:55: Item #1	
	7:05: Item #2	
	7:15: Item #3	
7:25	Communication	
7:30	Closing Prayer	Debbie Duncan

Next Meeting is (date)_____

Explanation and Responsibility of Agenda Items

Prayer

Each person on the board takes turns giving the opening prayer. As servant leaders and disciples, we need to become comfortable praying in a group. This may also be a time to ask for personal prayer requests from fellow leaders.

Spiritual Formation

Again, take turns allowing each member to share. Relate the devotion to the leadership equipping topic or something on the agenda if possible. Another option is a time of spiritual development related specifically to leadership. This might be a time to challenge leaders to share where they are seeing God at work in their lives this past week. This helps prepare them to share their faith in their day-to-day life. (See *Get Their Name* for more information on sharing your faith in small groups.)

This is a time to dive deep and help our leaders mature in their faith and grow in their knowledge. Do not glaze over this important time in the faith development of the board collectively and each member's individual spiritual journey. Bring topics that challenge the members and promote dialogue. Refer back to the list of topics created as suggestions for this time completed at the previous fall retreat. Allow about fifteen minutes.

Leadership Equipping

Yep, you guessed it. The responsibility for leadership equipping is shared. Rather than choosing a random subject, be intentional in brainstorming leadership equipping topics and resources developed at the strategic planning leadership retreat. Board members can then choose a topic or leadership book from the list, the group collectively decided to dive into, that the person leading the teaching time is passionate about. This approach provides ample preparation time, too. Make this an interactive time for the board. Do not shy away from challenging subjects or diving deep into subjects or materials. Remember, this time is to *develop and grow* our leaders who are modeling leadership for the congregation. Allow about fifteen minutes.

New People

Take a look at the report on the number of first and second-time guests. What is noticed? Are there improvements to celebrate? Are their gaps to be addressed? Questions of accountability and next steps will be directed to the pastor.

Goal Review and Accountability Conversation

Remember those annual goals set at the strategic planning retreat? The pastor will provide an update on the goal progress. Friends, this is really where the rubber hits the road! This is where accountability most likely will need to kick in through adaptive change. Board members are not likely experienced in the practice of holding their pastor accountable. If progress is lacking, ask about it. Talk about it! How can we be encouraging? What support is needed? Are there gaps in training or resources from either the pastor or staff? Is the pastor having trouble holding staff and leaders accountable and needs the board's help? If the goal progress is not on track, what progress is expected by the next meeting? Be specific in setting up expectations. Be sure to also acknowledge and celebrate progress and accomplishments!

Packet

This is the time of the meeting where items are reviewed and/or discussed from the packet that was sent out the week prior to the meeting. Questions or observations about vital signs would be discussed or reviewed at this time if needed. The usual method of working through most of the leadership packet is a Consent Calendar. A Consent Calendar methodology should include all the agenda items that a board needs to receive for archival reasons or to vote on for legal or *Book of Discipline* purposes. The minutes of the last meeting are an example of a consent calendar items. Other items could include the signing of a contract that has already been approved, or regular shifting of funds between accounts. The leader will ask if there are any corrections to the consent calendar agenda, or if anything needs to be removed from what is presented in the packet, for corrections or further discussion under *Generative and Strategic Work*, a future meeting, or by common agreement to adjust the agenda. If not, a covering motion for approval will be called for and seconded for all items that remain on the consent calendar. A vote to approve will then be taken. This is more of a formality than anything. Yet, it is important to have an accurate historical document of the governing decisions of the leadership council. For some items, especially financial matters and statistical data, a short oral description may prove very helpful. This also addresses the complexity of learning and processing styles among council members. The focus of any oral report should be to frame a fruitful and effective discussion. Beware, though, it is easy to get off track and start long discussions of items in the consent calendar. This voids its purpose and distracts the board from the more difficult, and more meaningful, strategic work of the board.

Generative and Strategic Work

While the previous two sections involved accountability to goals and understanding the church's health and missional fruitfulness, this agenda time may be used to reflect on the value of the goals themselves. What goals may need to be added, adapted, or changed to meet the changing ministry landscape and the needs of the mission field? What generative or strategic work is required to keep us in alignment to our mission and vision? What is changing in our culture that we need to adapt with in order to remain relevant to the people in our community we are trying to reach for Christ?

Chapter 10 offers a January through December flow of work for boards. Many of the items of focus in this annual calendar fit into this agenda item, including the annual pastor's assessment, budget preparation and the stewardship campaign, and organizing the strategic planning retreat. This type of work allows us to be proactive rather than reactive.

Additionally, reports or items pulled from the Consent Calendar may need to be discussed. There also could be an issue that brings about the need to establish a new guiding principle to allow ministry to happen without the leadership team's approval or intervention. It might be a new policy or manual is being created and needs to be reviewed and approved by the board. It might be an issue that could be handled by a guiding principle, but the principle has not been created and needs to be created. It could be a decision fell just outside a guiding principle and needs to be handled as an exception.

This portion of the agenda provides space and time for the board to address any places the leadership is stuck and needs to work through. This is time also for when individual team members may have questions, comments, concerns that need to be addressed for the overall good of the congregation as it pertains to church governance. Additionally, this is a time for leadership council members to ask for help from other team members on individual assignments from the board, such as the annual budget.

Keep alert that this time in the agenda does not become a catch-all for miscellaneous discussion with no structure or plan. Take time to get feedback from the board members so issues or questions can be placed on the agenda before your meeting so that the board's time can be used efficiently.

Communication

While a few items, such as personnel issues, require that the board go into executive session and the minutes preserved as confidential, the overwhelming majority of your board's business is designed to be shared. However, boards get so wrapped up in their discussion that they forget to take the important step of communicating their actions and strategic work to the larger congregation. That can quickly turn your members against the simplified structure, and reduce congregational trust. So, every meeting should end with a time to discuss your communication plan:

- What decisions were made tonight? This ensures everyone is on the same page and decisions are well documented in the minutes.
- Who needs to hear those decisions? What needs to be shared from this meeting?
- Who is responsible to communicate the decisions and when? How will the responsible person know about their responsibility to communicate if they are not at the leadership board table? What will be the methods used (email, newsletters, etc.)?
- How can the board support the ministry of the pastors, staff, and ministry teams by keeping the congregation abreast of the board's strategic priorities and work toward the church's mission?

Clarity about what should be communicated keeps the board on task, places the work of the board during the meeting in context, and connects the board to the larger congregation. See Chapter 9 on Communicating for a larger perspective on connecting the work of the leadership board to the larger church and community.

Prayer

Everyone takes turns providing the closing prayer. This is a great time to check-in with prayer partners, too (for information about leadership board prayer partners, see the section on leadership retreats in Chapter 10).

Checklist for Board Agenda Building

- Create an agenda that reflects your values, mission, and vision.

- Prepare the board packet and distribute a week in advance of meetings.

- Be vigilant about the agenda. Do not migrate back to the old model!

- Communicate! By simplifying your structure, you have considerably reduced the number of people "in the know," so you will need to increase your communications proportionally.

CHAPTER NINE

Communicating

Our church needs better communication! Have you ever heard this? It is rare to do any sort of consulting work in a church without hearing this from members and even some leaders. Some may roll their eyes when they hear this. Their perception is that people do not pay attention to what is said or what is printed. After all, it was the 47th item in the email blast and in the newsletter! Yes, it is true that communication is a two-way street. Yet, the burden of providing clear, distinct, and timely communication is on the church leadership. Effective communication builds trust and a sense of transparency. Trust and transparency are key in transitioning to simplified structure and modeling accountable leadership.

Communication must come from several different levels of the organization: board, pastor, staff, and ministry areas. We believe part of the common communication concerns come when the burden of communication is placed at only one or two levels. Certainly, there needs to be a communication hub (perhaps a communication coordinator or office administrator), but information needs to come in and go out at all levels.

If we can all agree that congregations need to do more to communicate, contemplate the communication effect of four or five committees worth of members being consolidated into one board. Your church may have been depending on those committee members to share the "business of the church" through casual conversations. Now that much fewer people are in the "room where it happens," so you will need to quadruple your communications just to stay even with your previous level which is already inadequate.

Because this resource is intended for boards moving to simplified accountable leadership, we will concentrate on communication responsibilities of the board. There are five communication strategies we ask you to consider: congregational conversations, newsletter articles, electronic communication, and commissioning of leadership.

Board Reporting

In our sample agenda for every board meeting, the last agenda item we suggest is communication. A simplified structure immediately becomes less accountable when others inside the congregation perceive the leadership board to be a secret group of insiders or the "pastor's buddies." As stated in Chapter 6, every meeting of the board needs to include a time of discussing what board actions or discussions need to be shared with the larger congregation, and how best does this message need to be shared. First, you may wish to make the leadership packet and minutes public for every member to read (except for executive session items, such as personnel matters). But beyond sharing minutes, how might the leadership board help to shape the congregation's Christ-centered purpose, its identity as an impactful faith community, and the congregation's ongoing narrative of faithfulness and fruitfulness before God? This chapter includes several suggestions, but we first recommend that leadership boards follow a slogan from the recovery community, "Take the cotton out of your ears and put it in your mouth." In other words, take time to listen – listen to God, listen to your fellow congregation members that who believe God is working through, and listen to the needs of the community.

Congregational Conversations

Sometimes we refer to congregational conversations as a "Town Hall Meeting," "Quarterly Conference," or a "State of the Church Address." Choose a name that is appropriate and appealing in your context. The important thing here is not in the title of the gathering, but in its practice. It is suggested to hold these quarterly as you transition into the simplified, accountable structure. As time goes by and the congregation becomes more comfortable with the model, the conversation frequency may need to be only a couple of times per year. The gathering is led by the board chair and/or other designee from the board. The pastor is in attendance, but does not lead the conversation. The purpose of the conversation is to build trust, continuously cast the vision, offer information to the congregation, receive feedback, and answer questions. Most all of the other communication strategies are one-way. Town halls and other congregational feedback opportunities offer the possibility for two-way conversations.

The format for this gathering is based on the governing focus of the board. This means the board would be presenting information on mission, vision, goals, and core values. The board might offer information on the alignment of the church around these. The board may also present the budget or perhaps a financial church overview. As you consider the rhythm of your town hall gatherings, here are some suggested areas of topics that relate to the seasons of the life of the congregation. At the beginning of the year, you could offer a town hall gathering to present the newly elected leadership team and to thank the outgoing team. This would also be the time to present the new budget and goals for the new year. During the second quarter of the year, you might provide an update on the progress made of the goals and the year to date financial report (overview, not details). During the third quarter, you would have the opportunity to not only update the congregation on the goal progress and financial reports, but you would gain information from the congregation to help the leaders discern the church goals for the upcoming year. During the fourth quarter, the opportunity is presented to celebrate the ministries, servants, and progress made through the goals to live into the vision. Use your knowledge of your congregation's annual flow and expectations to build a schedule that works for your context. Chapter 10 offers some other examples as well.

These congregational gatherings are not meant to be a place for people to come and air their frustrations or dirty laundry. Therefore, create a mission-focused environment by having an agenda and a stated time limit. When opening the meeting for questions, ask for questions around the specific topic in hand. For example, "What questions might you have about the goals set for this upcoming year?" If someone tries to hijack the meeting, goes off-topic, or is not speaking with respect, politely tell the person you will have a private conversation with them immediately following the meeting. You can also use tools, such as table talks where board members each facilitate a table discussion, to increase two-way communication while reducing the chance of one member attempting to "hijack" the conversation.

Newsletter Articles

We often leave the newsletter creation up to one person. It is often the sole responsibility of a single human being to write articles, lay out the newsletter, add graphics, and distribute. One central person being responsible for the layout and distribution makes great sense. Yet, it is important for the newsletter to reflect multiple thoughts, perspectives, ideas, and information from various areas of the church. This is a great place for the board/council to participate in the overall communication and transparency of the church. Assign various members of the board to contribute articles or information to the newsletter each month. Share what the board is working on and the progress made. Share general financial information. Share the celebrations of the church. Please do not depend only on the pastor for this leadership perspective. The board's missional focus and responsibility can be communicated using the newsletter.

Electronic Communication

In today's world, we must offer multiple engagement with social media and other electronic communication. This might include text, Facebook, email, Instagram, Twitter, etc. Find ways to engage the congregation through social media that matches the context of both your congregation as well as the new people you are trying to reach. Sometimes we limit our communication means to the preferences of only our members, when we are quite possibly missing the opportunity to communicate in more modern methods with new people. Again, do not limit this responsibility to only one person. The board may find it appropriate to use electronic communication from time to time to engage with the congregation. This might include newsy information, but it is also a chance to share a quote from a spiritual or leadership development time at the board meeting. It might also be a short Tweet about the record-breaking attendance at the Christmas Eve service(s) that everyone could celebrate. Be creative! Engage with your congregation!

Commissioning of Leadership

Lay leadership, especially lay governance, needs to be celebrated and lifted up as a valid form of ministry. In addition to all the informational sharing we recommend, another means to communicate with the congregation is through a service of commissioning during a Sunday morning worship. This could be right before or right after the new board goes into effect each year. Bringing the new board forward during worship allows the congregation to know the leaders of the church. It also gives the opportunity to offer a blessing and demonstrate gratitude for their service. This could be a time to sincerely thank those rolling off the board, too. The commissioning ritual is short, but clearly demonstrates the responsibility given and expected of the board.

Individual Conversations

As a member of the church's leadership board, you represent the church when having conversations with fellow congregants. Until your term ends, you are never not a board member. You also represent the church in your community. Make sure you are upholding a missional focus and the unified voice of the whole leadership board. You have an important role of being both a church and a Christian ambassador. People look to you to be a role model for the church. This does mean that you will need to set aside some of your personal agendas. During your term of service, you will need to represent not only the choir you sing in, the Sunday School class you lead, or your teenager's youth group. You are one of the representatives of the entire church, both inwardly to other congregation members and outwardly to the community. Conversations about the church need to keep Christ's mission and vision for the congregation in the forefront.

Checklist for Communicating

Use various forms of continuous communication:

- Congregational town halls and opportunities for two-way communication
- Newsletter contributions
- Social Media and other electronic communication
- Commission the board each year
- Individual conversations

CHAPTER TEN

A Year in Leadership

Before you know it, it is the end of the year AGAIN. It just slips up on you. We all have the best of intentions of making this upcoming year our best ever. Sometimes we even put some initial steps in place. Other times we have great intentions, but we just never quite launch the plan to make it happen. Time and time again, we see councils/boards set some really great goals for the year. They are worded *just so*. Then they are packed away ... until the end of the year. Then someone mentions them and we pull them back out to review. Upon review, we find we missed accomplishing our well-intentioned goals for the year. We simply did not keep them on the front burner directing our focus, time, and energy. We wanted them to happen, but we missed the intentionality in guiding our church towards the accomplishment of our goals. So, we encourage you to plan your year in leadership, keeping your goals in front of you the entire year, and being intentional on how you use your meeting time.

Leadership Rhythm

There is a natural rhythm to sound leadership. When a natural rhythm is discovered and practiced by the leadership board, then pastors, lay leaders, and the congregation are usually much more comfortable with a simplified accountable leadership structure. A natural rhythm provides much desired transparency and missional clarification. Sound rhythm helps manage healthy expectations, establish good communication methods, and sets a clear congregational direction. Rhythm promotes growth in leadership and spiritual maturity. This is vitally important since a congregational board partners with the pastor as spiritual leaders of the church.

The fiduciary, strategic, and generative functions of board governance is itself a rhythm. As you look at the annual flow of meeting topics in this chapter, notice how these three beats show up month after month as the board focuses on stewardship of resources (fiduciary work), makes plans and sets goals (strategic work), and creatively assesses its work toward fulfilling God's vision (generative work).

There is also a natural rhythm of the regular "church stuff" (i.e. pastoral review, budget preparation) we tend to year after year at specific times of the year. A new natural rhythm develops when we are able to artfully combine the new work of the simplified, accountable leadership (strategic, generative, and fiduciary) with the regular business of congregational life.

Has your church found its rhythm? Please allow us to offer some insights on the rhythm of leadership in the life of a church. We have found this rhythm to work with most churches, but feel free to adapt it to meet your needs and context. For instance, since your board probably includes the duties and responsibilities of the staff-parish relations committee, your annual conference may have specific due dates for assessment and consultation paperwork. Once leadership has found their rhythm, worship planning and ministry objectives will more likely be able to find their rhythm to sync with the leadership board.

January

Start the year with an intentional and well-organized orientation and formational time for new board members. This will also help the continuing board members "re-set" and be reminded about the congregation's vision, the principles of accountable leadership, and the mutual expectations of board members. There is a lot of organizational work to complete at this first meeting:

- This is a time of reviewing the expectations of leadership and practices of the board for new people.

- Set the board's calendar of meetings and retreats for the year.

- Finalize and have each board member sign the leadership covenant.

- At the first gathering of the new board and each subsequent year, the board will need to elect the "chair of trustees" as required by the *Book of Discipline*. It is recommended the board/council chair serve as the "chair of the trustees" for legal purposes. The Board of Trustees are considered the Board of Directors for purposes of incorporation with your secretary of state.

- A person will need to be named or a rotation will need to be set up for taking minutes at each meeting.

- Each board member could be assigned a month to communicate to the congregation through newsletters, social media, and/or worship. Use the opportunity to share about the general work of the board, offer spiritual equipping from a lay leader's perspective, and keep the board connected relationally and emotionally to the larger congregation.

• This is also a great time to assign responsibility for spiritual and leadership development times in the upcoming months of board meetings.

As you begin your new year, be sure to have a commissioning of service for the board in congregational worship if it was not done in December. The congregation needs to be able to see their leaders and this commissioning also serves as an opportunity to teach the congregation about the responsibilities of spiritual leadership.

February

Easter is coming! This would be a perfect time to ask accountability questions of your pastor around expectations of first-time guests and returning guests for the upcoming Lenten season. You also need to be sure to support the spiritual health of your board leaders. It is easy to focus on the business of doing church while forgetting that our real business is Jesus Christ. So, plan a spiritual retreat for the pastor and board to kick off the Lenten season. The spiritual retreat is a time for fasting, prayer, relationship building, and spiritual discernment.

At the end of January, your congregation submitted statistical end-of-year information on membership, ministry, and financial health. Your February meeting is a timely opportunity to compare trend lines over multiple years. Your district or conference office can get you charts that track annual statistics back over a decade. What is growing? What is shrinking? Where are the gaps? If you run a January-December financial year, you should have closed your books by the February meeting. Take the opportunity to look at the rhythm of giving and expenses over the year and be sure to fulfill your fiduciary responsibilities concerning church finances, taxes, apportionments, etc.

In order to get on contractor work schedules, midwinter is usually the best time to begin preparing for any needed facility improvements that may likely be completed during the spring or summer months.

March

It is a good idea to have three or four gatherings (i.e. Town Hall Meetings) with the congregation to keep lines of communication open and demonstrate transparent leadership. March might be a good time to schedule a congregational Town Hall, perhaps connected to your Lenten theme. Board members should share about the state of the church, pray together for the church's neighborhood mission field, celebrate wins, and give attendees a "sneak" peak into plans for Easter and upcoming summer ministries. Take some time for feedback, which could include intentional "table talk" (imagine several round tables with a different board member at each table, asking a set group of questions and doing intentional listening) or other methods that have proven to be fruitful in your context. The purpose of these town halls is to inform, encourage, and build trust.

April

With first quarter financial numbers now in, your board should assess the congregation's finances in greater detail. Is the church on stable footing as you begin to head into the summer months when giving is traditionally lower? What will the stewardship or generosity campaign be for this fall? Who will lead the campaign? What preparations need to be made? Is a temporary work team needed to help prepare with the pastor? Consider a time for the board to serve together in the community as an action of missional leadership and team-building.

May

Review policies and procedures. Are all job descriptions complete? Do any need to be updated or revised? Are there any updates needed in the employee manual? Are guiding principles in place (see Chapter 6)? Do any need to be revised or updated? Are the building usage policies updated? Are there any missing policies or procedures that would make everyday church life work more efficiently or effectively?

June

We are now halfway through the year. A more in-depth review of goals might be helpful. Are we on track to meet all goals? Where are the gaps? What shifts need to be made? Are more resources needed? Do we have the right personnel in the right place to accomplish the goals? How can the board be encouraging?

July is the usual time that new pastoral appointments often begin in the United Methodist Church. In our book, *IMPACT!: Reclaiming the Call of Lay Ministry*, we devote an entire chapter to the huge evangelism opportunity of receiving a new pastor, and offer some tips for leadership teams to be "co-owners" of the pastor transition process alongside a new pastor. If you are receiving a new pastor, the June meeting will probably be about supervising the work of various teams assigned particular tasks:

- Preparing a welcome celebration for new pastor and her family.
- Share a pastoral transition with wider community and local media as an evangelism opportunity.
- Organizing a process of intentional relationship building and orientation through cottage meetings or listening sessions with congregation members for July, August, and September.
- Scheduling a series of appointments for the new pastor to meet with community leaders and strategic church members.
- Working with the current and incoming pastor to share information, congregational metrics, and community demographics.

July

As the Nominations Committee begins to meet, what gifts would be helpful for the board members to have in the next season of the church's life? Notify the Committee of requests the board might have. What would a potential new board member need to know about the commitment and expectations of being a board member before accepting the nomination? Evangelism opportunities are coming up, so ask accountability questions of the lead pastor around plans on reaching new people during the Back-to-School and Advent seasons.

This might be the time for another Town Hall meeting. While not usually a "high attendance" month in many churches, July could provide a time for your board to engage your deeply engaged members and leaders. Use this time to gather information, such as community opportunities to reach new people, ideas for to launch or grow ministries, and gauge what areas might bring excitement or passion. Use the information you get during your upcoming fall board planning retreat to set your upcoming goals and priorities.

If you have received a new pastor, use the July meeting to help the pastor understand how your church is using the simplified, accountable leadership structure. It is one thing to see the single board on a piece of paper, it is quite another to experience it in practice. The enculturation of a new pastor to the church's mission and vision, the congregation's guiding principles, the concepts of accountable leadership, and the board's template agenda is all squarely the responsibility of the governing board in its capacity as both the church council and the staff-parish relations committee.

August

This is a very important month! The board will be making final preparations for the leadership retreat and conducting the retreat in August or early September. Are staff evaluations complete and any compensation change requests received from the pastor for budgetary considerations?

If you have received a new pastor, the listening sessions or cottage meetings should be in full swing. What has your new pastor learned about the congregation? Also, district superintendents often will check-in with the board chair (if this is also the SPRC contact) to inquire how the first few weeks of the new appointment are going. How is the board helping your new pastor connect to the congregation, to community leaders, and to the larger mission field?

September

The leadership strategic planning retreat will be conducted. (Note: budget accordingly.) The retreat is led by the chair with assistance from the pastor. There will be a time of review and analysis of the current year as well as planning for the upcoming year. The end of this chapter outlines more about the retreat and its objectives, but please note that the "work product" of a leadership retreat is about so much more than just getting plans on paper. The retreat is a time for team building. It is also a time of play and fun. Do not forget to begin work on the new leadership covenant for the upcoming year. Your team has learned a lot over the past several months about how to be healthy, accountable leaders of your faith community. Use some time to make sure your learnings are incorporated into the covenant.

In many annual conferences, early fall is when you begin work on your charge conference documents. Work teams may need to be deployed to work on different aspects of the report, and that means you may assign a board member or two to get assistance from church members or staff with expertise outside the board to complete different portions such as the facilities and finance reports. Eventually, your entire board will need to approve and recommend the charge conference packet to the charge conference. The board will also need to coordinate with the independent Committee on Nominations and Leadership Development on preparing the slate of new board members for approval at the charge conference. Chapter 5 offers some tips to assist your nominating committee in fulfilling this important task.

October

Depending on your annual conference calendar, this may be the time of year for the pastor's evaluation by the board to be submitted to the District Superintendent. Since a goal evaluation was completed the month prior at the retreat, the board is now fully prepared for the evaluation. The board has evaluative information rather than personal preferences for the basis of the evaluation. After the upcoming year's God-sized goals are set at the leadership strategic planning retreat, the pastor will be working on the objectives with the staff and ministry teams. This is most likely in an off-site staff retreat. (Note: Budget accordingly.) Once the objectives are set, budget requests can be made available to the board for consideration. The second Sunday in October is clergy appreciation day. How will the board acknowledge and celebrate their clergy? How are the staff, ministry leaders, and other servant leaders celebrated?

November

The upcoming year's budget needs to be in its final revisions based on the stewardship campaign and the staff/ministry team leaders' requests. This might be the charge conference month if you have not already had one in October. How is your budget aligning with the mission, vision, and strategic goals of the church? If you are not funding your God-sized goals, then it will be very hard to hold your pastor accountable to the results.

December

In early December, it is a great time to hold a "state of the church" gathering with the congregation. This is a time to review the year and share goals for the upcoming year. Celebrate the fruitful ministries and accomplishments of the year!

In December or January, your board will probably need to complete consultation documents for the bishop and cabinet, in consideration of the pastor's appointment. This work is both sacred and confidential. Only elected board members who are identified as staff/pastor-parish relations committee (S/PPRC) members should be present in discussions and the eventual vote recommending that your pastor return or move.

The Annual Strategic Planning Retreat

There are those that might cringe (maybe you did just now) at the thought of a leadership retreat. But allow us to challenge you a bit. In our experience, this can be one of the most transformational times in the life of the board and thus the congregation. The focused time away evaluating the current year and seeking discernment on its leadership of the upcoming year is absolutely critical. Without this crucial gathering time, we find boards have more difficulty with focused leadership. Those boards that have gotten into the rhythm of annual leadership retreats have not only begun to look forward to them, but they are great fun that builds excitement for the entire church.

As best practices, we offer a couple of thoughts for your consideration in planning your annual leadership retreat. First, make sure the date goes on your board members' calendar early. Stress the importance of each and every member attending. All voices and thoughts matter! Second, we highly recommend taking the board away from the church for the retreat. Make it an overnight experience if possible. Ideally, we find a 24-hour experience from Friday night through Saturday to work best for most. Incorporate some team building exercises and playing together into the agenda. I also like to assign prayer partners the week or two leading up to and during the retreat. Plan times for prayer partners to pray with and for one another at the retreat, too. Third, we recommend having an outsider facilitate your retreat if possible. Someone leading the group from outside allows everyone (including the pastor and all board members) to be able to participate more fully without having to lead. This allows more of an immersion opportunity for everyone.

Chapter 7 lists the five primary components of strategic ministry planning that will guide your work:

- Mission
- Vision
- Core Values
- God-sized Goals
- Objectives/Strategies

Retreat Objectives

At the strategic planning retreat, evaluate the church's impact in reaching the mission. How many new people are coming to know Jesus Christ through the life of the congregation? How are people growing in their faith? Take some time at the retreat for spiritual discernment amongst the leadership team members field. How is the board discerning God's will and direction for the church? How is each member individually and collectively spending time with God throughout the year in this discernment? Are any shifts needed in the leadership direction because of the team discernment?

Next, review the vision statement. The vision statement should be a guiding focus for the congregation. It should provide energy and momentum. Is the vision statement now a reality? Is it time for a new vision statement? What led you to that conclusion? It is often helpful to review the life cycle of your church to evaluate the vision's effectiveness in driving the church. Vision is needed for a growing church. If vision is not driving your church, it will soon be in decline or further decline. We recommend familiarizing yourself with the Bullard Life Cycle of the Church and using it for a vision evaluation. It can be found in various online sites, including some materials Kay has prepared to assist team that are located on www.blakebradford.org.

Now review the current year's goals. God-sized goals are evaluated monthly with the pastor at the board meetings, but this is a time to dive deeper. A great deal of the time at the retreat will be spent on setting goals for the upcoming year. Discuss what steps need to be taken to live into the vision of the church and to be more faithful in its mission. Typically, there are three to five overall church goals identified each year.

Consider what training might be needed. What gaps were identified in meetings on topics discussed by the board in the previous year? What topics are missing completely? Are the new board members familiar with the structure, policies, responsibilities, etc.? Bring in outside information or trainers, if needed, to make sure everyone is up to speed on what they need to know and so that every board member is equipped to be the best possible leader for the church.

Allow us to offer a friendly reminder. Creating strategies/objectives are not the work of the leadership board.

This is the work of the staff and ministry leaders. If you are talking specific ministries or dates, you are managing and not governing. Stay out of the weeds of management! Your job as the leadership board is to discern the congregation's purposeful *why* and define *where* the church needs to head to be faithful. *What* and *how* is the responsibility of the staff and ministry team leaders.

Spiritual and Prayer Time at the Retreat

Spend some in-depth time in spiritual development with the board. This might include a time unpacking the difference of being a secular leader versus being a church leader. What scripture might be helpful in diving deep into these distinctions? Have the board share where they are in their spiritual journey. Ask them to suggest spiritual development topics they would like to spend time on during the monthly spiritual development times. Ask each member to commit to an area of spiritual growth in the upcoming year. This whole process may be uncomfortable for some leaders. This may be the first time these types of questions and conversations have taken place. Be patient and grace-filled around this conversation. After all, we are all growing as disciples in our own ways. However, do not shy away from it. Again, these are your spiritual leaders of the church and it is important to help them grow and mature in their faith and model it for others.

Prayer is an essential part of the retreat experience. You might pair people up as prayer partners leading into the retreat and during the retreat. Some boards even maintain their prayer partner for the upcoming year. This is also an opportunity to have an accountability partner. Spend time in the retreat all praying aloud, praying in silence, and sharing prayers for one another. If possible, have the team go on a prayer walk. You might ask them to spend time seeking God's direction for the church in the upcoming year. Ask them to consider seeking God's will for their leadership in the upcoming year. I (Kay) have even asked leaders to find something in nature that reflects the future of the church and bring it (or a picture of it) back to share with the rest of the team. If you have leaders who are a bit uncomfortable with prayer, you might even include a teaching time on the different types of prayers. Be creative with this time, but do not overlook the importance of bathing the entire retreat in prayer. You might even consider launching a prayer initiative with the board that will be used for the entire congregation in the upcoming year. For example, check out Sue Nilson-Kibbey's book, *Flood Gates*, and her breakthrough prayer initiatives.

At the retreat, spend some time developing the leadership capabilities and understanding of your board. Also, take some time to identify gaps in leadership knowledge or practices that the board would like to learn about in the coming year. Make a list of topics and resources. These lists will be used to design leadership development time for the monthly board meetings.

Checklist for Planning Your Leadership Rhythm

- Establish your leadership rhythm and tweak it as necessary.

- Always plan at least one season ahead (bonus points for planning a year ahead!).

- Conduct at least one strategic planning leadership retreat annually.

- Evaluate mission, vision, and progress on goals monthly.

Conclusion

In the course of a few months, the church had been
through a consultation process, a lightning strike, an
assault on a board member in the facility, and a building
flood. The consultation team offered some very adaptive
recommendations dealing with worship, leadership development, and faith development among others. The lightning
strike affected the alarm system, Internet, and some of the
electronic equipment. The personal assault was horrific
for the board member and set a whole new security process
in motion. The flood was only a few inches, but it created
enough damage that the church had to relocate to another
facility for a few months while repairs were made. You could
say this church had a bad year of unfortunate circumstances.
Yet, in the midst of all of this, the pastor reported to me (Kay)
the silver lining. As part of the consultation, there was a
recommendation for the church to move to a simplified structure with accountable leadership. With all of the happenings
at the church, the pastor could not have imagined trying to
maneuver through four different administrative teams in a
timely manner to manage all the processes, decisions, and
new policies needed. The numerous situations the church
had to deal with certainly tested the new structure. But the

pastor emphatically believes the simplified structure not only allows them to maneuver through the situations with greater ease, focus, and timeliness, but this change was what he was most excited about. He believes it has changed the whole trajectory of the church and has given more intention and focus to his own leadership.

Remember the Why

Simplified, accountable structure is not the potential "magic bullet" some churches are searching for to suddenly create an avalanche of people coming in the doors. We hope this was not your expectation. Yet, in our experience, when we have a simplified means of being focused on our purpose, the mission is certainly possible. Simplified, accountable leadership is a means to re-focus the church on its purpose in a modern, efficient, and effective manner. We circle back to your motivation. Why does your church desire this change? If the change is the hope of a magic pill, you have come to the wrong place. If the change is being considered as a means to be more faithful at making disciples of Jesus Christ for the transformation of the world, we offer hope, prayers, and resources for this journey.

> *"Out of complexity, find simplicity."*
> **Albert Einstein**

We believe that Jesus called for the formation of "church" in his teachings. By church, we believe he meant a place where people could learn about God, worship God, and hold one another responsible for their faith walk. In our efforts to do this, we believe well-meaning leaders have unnecessarily complicated our churches' practices. Now, please

145

do not hear that we are suggesting this from a theological perspective, doctrine, or conviction – quite the contrary. What we are suggesting is that in our efforts to "do church" we have perhaps created systems and processes that have complicated church needlessly. Simplification of the structure allows us to focus back on the basics, which is making disciples. Simplification does not mean easy, but it is a clear, distinct pathway. Simplification allows us to return and focus upon the basic essentials of church. It reconnects authority and responsibility. Laity are unleashed from the meeting room to make an impact in the mission field. With the adaptive changes of simplification and accountability, we will once again become better focused on our true purpose – our *why* of being church. When we focus on our purpose, we can align our resources to be faithful to living out our mission of making new disciples.

It is our prayer that your church is both challenged and excited about the potential outcomes of this journey. Be patient with one another. It will take time to "live into" simplified, accountable leadership. But, oh, the efforts are worth it! Be blessed in this time of moving closer to faithful effectiveness in reaching new people for Christ so your church can claim:

Mission Accomplished!

Epilogue
to the First Edition

There is a cultural movement toward simplification. Think of the "tiny house" phenomenon where people move to a simpler, scaled-down lifestyle. People crave less hassle in a streamlined, simplified fashion in which to go about life today. People have little patience for the complicated, layered, and time-intensive. This book is an attempt to help the church adapt to simplification for the culture of today. Through this simplification, the church is then able to focus on its purpose. By removing all the unnecessary layers and becoming accountable to making disciples, a church has a better chance of reaching new people for Jesus Christ. We would have trouble identifying a church that is growing and reaching new people that has not simplified their structure!

Your church form matters. Your church footprint matters. Your church function matters. Your church structure matters. American architect, Louis Sullivan, coined the phrase, "form ever follows function." Here is how he explains the "law:"

*"Whether it be the sweeping eagle in his flight, or the open apple-blossom, the toiling work-horse, the blithe swan, the branching oak, the winding stream at its base, the drifting clouds, over all the coursing sun, **form ever follows function**, and this is the law. Where function does not change, form does*

not change. The granite rocks, the ever-brooding hills, remain for ages; the lightning lives, comes into shape, and dies, in a twinkling. It is the pervading law of all things organic and inorganic, of all things physical and metaphysical, of all things human and all things superhuman, of all true manifestations of the head, of the heart, of the soul, that the life is recognizable in its expression, **that form ever follows function.** *This is the law."*[1]

In other words, Sullivan believed that the purpose trumps the design. The building (structure) needs to be built to serve the function (purpose/mission) of the building, not the other way around. Too many times our churched get stuck in the tradition and methods rather than boiling the way we function down to foremost serving its purpose. Sullivan's teaching helps remind us that how we structure (our form) should follow the ideal way to be about the mission (function). Indeed, our structure matters!

Sometimes our structure limits our ability. We may have all the passion in the world without the ability to call a play. We may have no way to huddle together to communicate the play. Complicated structure can limit our communications and generate misunderstandings. Sometimes our structure actually creates confusion rather than provide direction. The way our church is structured can hold us back from being effective. Our very structure sometimes sets us up to fumble the ball time and time again. Indeed, your structure matters.

While structure is extremely important, it is not the end-all, be-all solution. Forming a new structure is not the magic bullet. Just streamlining structure in your church will not automatically create an influx of new people coming to know Jesus. Getting your structure right is not the prescription to make all right again.

---

1 Sullivan, Louis H. (1896). "The Tall Office Building Artistically Considered." Lippincott's Magazine (March 1896): 403–409.

Restructuring is not the first thing you tackle either. Changing your structure is not the starting point. You must first get mission and vision straight. Get fired up with radical hospitality. Provide a "wow" worship experience. Ensure you have a vibrant children, youth, and young adult ministry. Get your connection, discipleship, and leadership processes in place. Structure is important, but structure is not where transformation begins.

Yet, eventually you will need to address your structure. There is no organization to point to that if they are successful at their mission, they have not spent time on aligning their structure. We must simply structure for the purpose of accomplishing the mission. The mission will not be accomplished without intentional structural alignment to allow the mission to happen.

We hope this book helps you understand at least one way to simplify church structure and how to make it work. But remember, it is just one model. It is not the only model. There may be other ways to simplify, but this is the way we have found to do this in the United Methodist Church. The real key is to simplify. This is all about simplifying to align all to the purpose of making disciples.

Our hope and prayer is that this resource when coupled with our previous resources, will be helpful in your church reaching your community in effective ways for Jesus Christ for the transformation of the world.

Bishop Robert Farr
Missouri Annual Conference
The United Methodist Church

Appendices

APPENDIX A

Simplified Accountable Leadership Structure
Frequently Asked Questions

1. Which positions can be combined for one person on the Board to hold?

Most all positions can be combined as long as the minimum number are elected. The Lay Leader, Lay Delegate, PPR Chair, and Trustee Chair must be designated, but could all be the same person.

2. Is there an absolute minimum number for the Board?

Nine

3. Does the pastor have a vote?

No

4. Can family members serve together on the Board?

Per the *Book of Discipline,* family members cannot serve on the Board together. If it cannot be avoided, the family members may need to excuse themselves from the room or not vote on issues with potential conflict of interest. Staff and family of staff cannot serve on the Board.

5. Should staff (paid and unpaid) serve on the Board?

No

6. Who should take notes at the meeting?

Someone can be assigned or elected to take notes who is not on the Board. That person could be elected from the existing members of the Board, a person recruited outside the Board to take notes (needs to be excluded from PPR conversations), or a person who is an addition to the Board with the sole responsibility of taking notes.

7. Are the Financial Secretary and Treasurer required to be on the Board?

No, but they can be. A best practice is for them not to be on the Board.

8. Which position on the Board serves as the liaison to the District Superintendent for Staff/Pastor Parish Relations Committee purposes?

It is recommended that the Board Chair serves as the S/PPRC liaison to the DS.

9. Are there still three-year terms and classes?

Yes. One third of the Board will roll off each year.

10. Is the Board self-nominating?

No. There is still a requirement that there be a separate Committee on Nominations and Leadership Development to nominate the Board Members to the Charge Conference each year.

11. How long can a person serve on the Board? Can they roll from three years as Trustee specialist to three years as a Finance specialist?

Board members serve a three-year term. Since all specialists are also serving as PPR, Trustees, and Finance, it is recommended they roll off after each three-year term. After being off the Board for a year, the person can roll back onto the Board if elected. The Lay Leader and Lay Member to Annual Conference are exempt from the three-year term.

12. Are UMM, UMW, and UMYF representatives required to be on the Board?

Your governing documents and nominations report approved by the Charge Conference will make that decision. If the church has these chartered groups, a member of that group may serve if requested on the Board as elected by their chartering group. It is not a requirement if the group decides not to elect a representative.

13. How many must be present to take an official vote? What requires an official vote?

A quorum is described as whoever is present for a duly called meeting, with a simple majority of those attending rules. The one exception to the quorum rule is when the Leadership Board is taking official action as the Board of Trustees (or legal Board of Directors for state civil matters). In that case, a quorum may be constituted by a majority of the members of the board.

14. How is the Trustee Chair elected or appointed as required by the corporate resolution?

At the first meeting at the beginning of each new year, the Board will elect a Trustee Chair to satisfy the corporate resolution requirement. It is recommended the Board Chair serve as the Trustee Chair. Please note that all members of the board who will serve as trustees must be of legal age (eighteen or over in most states).

15. If a church moves to the simplified structure, how does ministry happen?

Even though the restructuring occurs, ministry teams are still needed and in place. Fewer people on the Board means more people are available to do ministry. Simplifying structure is the combining of the four administrative teams of the Council, Trustees, Finance Committee, and S/PPRC. Governance restructuring does not necessarily affect ministry teams.

16. Do I need approval from my District Superintendent to move to the simplified structure?

Yes. Consultation and a letter from the pastor requesting to move to simplified structure to the DS are some of the first steps. In the letter, state the missional purpose of moving to this structure.

17. Where can I find information on simplified structure in the Book of Discipline?

Paragraph 247.1 in the 2016 edition.

APPENDIX B

Ten Steps to Transition to Simplified, Accountable Leadership Structure

DATE   **STEP**

_____ 1. Determine why a structure change is needed or desired. Equip your leaders in basic principles of discernment and accountable leadership. Create a draft time line and plan for discernment, communication of the proposed change, congregational votes, and launch.

_____ 2. Consult your District Superintendent for a preliminary conversation about a potential structure change.

_____ 3. Ensure the congregation is prepared for an accountable leadership model of governance. Prepare for and lead congregational conversations about potential changes utilizing two-way communication. Lead with the why and then follow with the "what" and "how."

_____ 4. Uncover and discuss feedback from congregation and use the feedback to build your model for a new leadership structure.

_____ 5. Create a temporary task force, approved by the existing administrative board or church council, to create a draft set of founding guiding principles, and to begin preparing updates for all existing congregational policies (personnel, facility, finance, endowment, by-laws, etc.) so that the policies will be in compliance with the proposed structure.

_____ 6. Letter to District Superintendent officially requesting a structure change and the convening of a Charge (Church) Conference.

_____ 7. The Committee on Nominations and Lay Leadership assembles to nominate new leaders illustrating new leadership criteria and structure.

154

_____ 8. The congregation's Charge Conference, preferably one convened as a Church Conference, is called with proper notice to approve:

- New structure

- Nominations

- A founding set of guiding principles that the new board is authorized to adapt to meet the ministry and missional needs of the church.

_____ 9. Congregational vote of the Charge or Church Conference. Once approved, all existing administrative teams cease to exist as separate bodies (this does not include ministry teams) on a certain date set by the Charge Conference. The responsibilities and authority of the constituent bodies will rest in the new board.

_____ 10. First meeting of the new board. Elect a trustee chair, orient the board on the guiding principles, and approve a board covenant.

APPENDIX C: Rules to Remember

All the *Disciplinary* requirements and limitations of each of the new Leadership Board's constituent committees remains in effect. Rules to remember:

1. A separate **Nominations Committee**, chaired by the Pastor, is required because the Board cannot self-nominate.

2. You will need **nine to fifteen** members. Board members serve a **three-year term**. The Lay Leader and Lay Delegate are exempt from the three-year term. After being off the Board for a year, the person can roll back onto the Board if elected. SPRC and Trustees have minimum and maximum limits on the number of members, so (depending on your Leadership Team's size and composition), a few members of the Leadership Team may be barred as voting members of some of the constituent committees. For instance, there is a limit of nine on Trustees. There is also a limit of eleven on SPRC, counting Lay Leader and a Lay Member of Annual Conference.

3. Pay attention to *Disciplinary* **conflicts of interest**. Household members cannot serve on the Board together. If it cannot be avoided, the family members may need to excuse themselves from the room or not vote on issues with potential conflict of interest. Staff and family of staff cannot serve on the Board because of SPRC membership restrictions (plus it is simply good ethics!).

4. Trustee Requirements: During the first meeting at the beginning of each new year, the Board will elect a Trustee Chair to satisfy the corporate resolution requirement. It is recommended the Board Chair serve as the Trustee Chair, if the Board chair is one of the Trustees. The Leadership Board, serving as the Trustees, is also the legal Board of Directors. All Board members who serve as Trustees must be over eighteen. The Trustee membership rule of minimum one-third laymen and one-third lay women remains in effect. The Pastor cannot be a Trustee.

5. Even though the restructuring occurs, **ministry teams** are still needed and in place. Fewer people on the Board means more people are available to do ministry. Simplifying structure is the combining of the four administrative teams of the Council, Trustees, Finance, and SPR Committees. The nurture, outreach, and witnessing ministries continue their disciple-making work.

6. The concept of a Leadership Board is **designed to increase accountability and alignment** for the whole church towards its holistic mission, not be a place for ministry representatives to negotiate "turf." Members of the Board only represent and lead the whole church, not a particular interest group or ministry.

7. While the Leadership Board **may designate specialists** (such as finance specialists) from the membership of their Board, the whole Board, *in toto*, serves as the finance committee, Trustees, etc., not just the designated specialists.

8. The small number of governance officers on the Leadership Board **requires huge trust and congregation-wide accountability**. It is HIGHLY RECOMMENDED that you describe your future Charge Conference as being "The Leadership Board, Nominations Committee, Treasurer and Finance Secretary (if non-staff) and all clergy who hold their charge conference in the congregation." It would also greatly help build trust, accountability, and transparency if your governing documents adopt a recommendation that asks the District Superintendent to convene all Charge Conferences as Church Conferences to allow all professing members to vote on matters. This allows the larger congregation to have a say in nominations and hold the Leadership Board accountable in the Board's role as the Charge Conference's executive committee.

9. Churches on **multi-point charges** will particularly need to take care to support and respect the organizational structure and ministry of one another's churches.

APPENDIX D
Organizational Charts

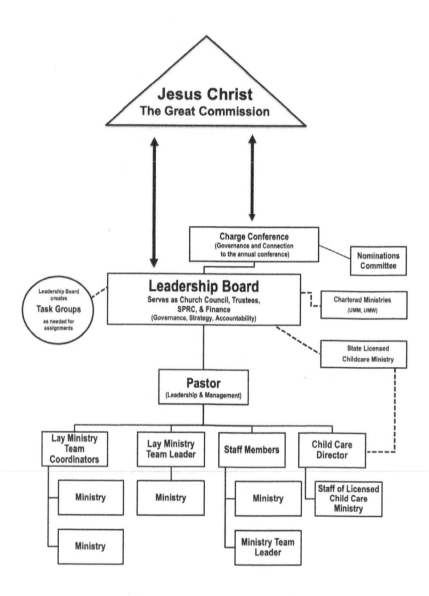

Alternate Model:
A "Dual Election" S/PPRC

Leadership Board contains 3-4 member of the Staff/Pastor Parish Relations Committee (one for each "class" year), including Chair and Lay Leader who serve dual roles both on the S/PPRC and on the Leadership Board. There are then additional S/PPRC members elected. S/PPRC continues to report to Leadership Board as it would to a Church Council.

LEADERSHIP BOARD

- Governance, Accountability and Strategy
- Serves as the Church Council, Trustees, & Finance Committee

S/PPRC

- Reports to Leadership Board
- Governance & Staffing Accountability

Pros:
- Creates stronger checks & balances in the governance, especially in congregations that have trust issues

- Multiple S/PPRC members on the Board make for stronger shared vision than having a totally separate S/PPRC

- This model can fill the needs of a Charge or Cooperative Parish S/PPRC

- Some District Superintendents require a separate, more independent S/PPRC.

Cons:
- The shared Board members who are also on S/PPRC can create authority issues and operational vagueness

- Separate S/PPRC dilutes the efficiency and accountability of the Leadership Board

- Pastor can receive mixed messages about priorities.

APPENDIX E
Board Application

This application from is adapted from the interest form created and used by the nominating committee of Camp Hill United Methodist Church of Camp Hill, Pennsylvania, to recruit and interview applicants to serve on their Unified Leadership Council.

The first year, you may need to use a mix of this interest form and some method of receiving recommendations from church members to create a pool of possible leaders. As your congregation grows in its experience of the benefits of a simplified accountable leadership structure and more disciples are unleashed for ministry, those gifted for governance leadership will be more readily identified.

You may wish to use this interest form alongside your leadership development process.

LEADERSHIP BOARD INTEREST FORM
Anytown United Methodist Church

First Name: _____

Last Name: _____

Preferred Phone Number: _____

Preferred Email Address: _____

Please write a brief paragraph about your family & vocational life (approx. 3 full sentences):

Please share a little about your spiritual journey & what you are currently most passionate about in ministry. Please limit the story to one paragraph (approx. 4 full sentences):

Please share why you feel called to be a part of the Leadership Board in one brief paragraph (approx. 3 full sentences):

Which worship service do you typically attend?

❑ 9:00am Traditional   ❑ 11:30am Contemporary

Are you part of a Sunday School Class or Wesleyan Small Group for discipleship? If so, which one?

❑ Gathering   ❑ Cornerstone   ❑ Celebration Choir

❑ New Beginning   ❑ Genesis   ❑ 20/30 Group

❑ College & Career   ❑ Forum   ❑ Journey Group

❑ Other:_____

Are you willing to serve a three-year term (January 2020 – December 2022)?

❑ Yes   ❑ No

If no, what length of time would you be willing to serve? _____

Are you available for a leadership retreat on September (DATE)?

❑ Yes   ❑ No

Please fill out this Interest Form completely and return to the church office or the welcome desk by___(DATE)___.

APPENDIX F

Sample Nominations Officiary Report
2020 Anytown First UMC Leadership

- Anytown United Methodist Church is governed according to the denomination's prescribed structure as found in the *United Methodist Book of Discipline*. All *Book of Discipline* and congregational policy references to the Church Council, Board of Trustees, Staff/Pastor Parish Relations Committee, Endowment Committee, and Finance Committee shall be understood to refer to the Leadership Board. Where years are listed, they represent the final year of an individual's term.

- The Nominations Committee has undertaken a careful and discerning process of preparing the slate below for approval by Church Conference. The committee's aim is to match persons with open positions according to the following considerations:

  o Maturity as a Disciple of Jesus Christ

  o Alignment with the church's mission: "Making Disciples of Jesus Christ for the Transformation of the world"

  o Length of membership tenure at Anytown UMC, with a balancing of experience in leadership with welcoming and engaging new leaders

  o Actively fulfilling member expectations (UM Discipline ¶217): prayers, presence, gifts, service, and witness

  o Past history of leadership in small groups, classes, ministry teams, and committees

- o Balance and diversity of the committee, particularly with age, gender, and areas of involvement

- o Ability to fulfill board requirements, the Board Covenant, and actively participate in meetings.

- As part of our Intentional Leadership Pathway, in *YEAR*, a class of "Preparatory Members" was created who will serve one year with voice, but without vote in order to prepare those who *may* subsequently be elected to serve a three-year voting term. In the event of a vacancy, the preparatory board member may be asked to complete a term.

Anytown FUMC Charge Conference

- The Charge Conference includes the members of the Leadership Board, the Nominations Committee, pastors appointed to the congregation, and all active and retired clergy who have designated our congregation as their home Charge Conference.

- In order to "encourage broader participation by members of the church, the nominations committee recommends that Anytown FUMC request that any annual or called Charge Conference be convened as a Church Conference to extend the vote to all professing members of the congregation (2016 *BOD* ¶248).

- The Leadership Board serves as the incorporated institution's board of directors and serves as the executive committee of the Charge Conference.

Leadership Board

The Leadership Board serves as the Church Council, SPRC,
Trustees, and Finance Committee of Anytown FUMC

Version with NINE on the Board:

Class of 2020
John Jones, T/F/SPR

Carol Clark, T/F/SPR/LM

Yolanda Youngperson, F/SPR/Y

Class of 2021
Jennifer Jackson, T/F/SPR/C

Ben Black, T/F/SPR/LL

Larry Lewis, T/F/SPR

Class of 2022
Sue Smith, T/F/SPR/UMW

David Dent, T/F/SPR/UMM

Debbie Duncan, T/F/SPR

Version with ELEVEN voting on the Board

(Includes separate Lay Leader and Lay Member of AC who
are not disciplinary term-limited)

Class of 2020
John Jones, T/F/SPR

Yolanda Youngperson, F/SPR/Y

Mary Miller, T/F/SPR

Class of 2021
Jennifer Jackson, T/F/SPR/C

Larry Lewis, T/F/SPR

Ron Roberts, T/F/SPR/Treasurer

Class of 2022
Sue Smith, T/F/SPR/UMW

David Dent, T/F/SPR/UMM

Debbie Duncan, T/F/SPR

Preparatory Member
Andrea Anderson (non-voting)

Ex-Officio Members:
Lay Leader: Ben Black, F/SPR/LL

Lay Member of AC: Carol Clark, F/SPR/LM

Key

T – Trustee (min five and max nine, and includes at least one-third men and at least one-third women)

SPRC – Staff Parish Relations Committee, (min three and max nine, not including the Lay Leader and Lay Member to Annual Conference who are members)

F – Finance

LM – Lay Member to Annual Conference (Ex Officio on SPRC)

LL – Lay Leader (Ex Officio on SPRC)

C – Chair

UMM – United Methodist Men

UMW – United Methodist Women

Y – Youth (*Note: members under eighteen cannot be an elected Trustee*)

Notes:

- At January meeting, Leadership Team will elect a Trustee Chairperson, which may be the Leadership Board Chairperson.
- Leadership Team may assign team members as Primary Contacts for matters pertaining to building maintenance, personnel, financial matters, or other areas of responsibility, but the Leadership Team operates as a single body encompassing the responsibilities of SPRC, Finance Committee, Endowment Committee, and Trustees.

Nominations Committee

Chairperson is the Appointed Senior Pastor (max nine members, not including the pastor)

Class of 2020	Class of 2021	Class of 2022
Carl Clark	Rollie Rich	Sally Smith
Belle Brady	Gene Galloway	Rob Roberts

Child Enrichment Weekday Ministry Advisory Board

Anytown FUMC's tuition-based ministries provide Christian care and education for children throughout the year. The respective advisory committees provide advisory support for our state-licensed ministries for children, and are subordinate to the Leadership Board of the congregation, according to UMC *Book of Discipline* ¶256.2.c. Since Anytown FUMC's weekday ministry shares the IRS employer ID number and nonprofit incorporation status with the church as a subordinate entity, the Anytown FUMC Nominations Committee recommends all the Advisory Board members and chair for election by the Charge Conference. Non-members of FUMC, such as parents, may be elected to the Advisory Board, but the chair, selected by the Nominations Committee, must be a member. A majority of Advisory Board members must be professing members of Anytown FUMC.

¶256.2.c. Weekday Ministry Board—The term weekday ministry applies to any regularly planned ministry for children. When appropriate, one or more weekday ministry boards may be organized to oversee the weekday ministry programs of the congregation. The board's membership should be mostly professing members of the congregation, with parent, church staff, and weekday ministry staff representatives. The board will set policies consistent with the congregation's policies, state mandates, and sound business practices. The board will guide weekday ministries as appropriate on opportunities for faith development, mission outreach, Christian education, evangelism, and safety. They will advocate for inclusion of children from various socioeconomic, cultural, and racial/ ethnic backgrounds. Weekday ministry board(s) accountability should be placed within the local church organizational structure with consideration to the group responsible for the congregation's education ministry.

Chairperson: Mary McMillan

Treasurer: *Chosen by Committee*

Secretary: *Chosen by Committee*

Class of 2020	Class of 2021	Class of 2022
Roland Rogers	Angela Atkins	Jeremy James
Suzy Simmons	Regina Rogers	Frankie Fulbright

Ex-Officio Members (with vote):

Director of Child Enrichment Ministries

Director of Faith Development

Senior Pastor

Associate Pastor

NOTES for Readers:

- We have included a sample of a non-independent child care ministry to the nominations report because these entities are often a source of questions. If your congregation's child care ministry is a separately incorporated 501(c)3, then a different kind of governing relationship must be explicitly negotiated and outlined. Take care to update any existing policies and by-laws so that the Leadership Team is defined as the executive committee of the congregation's Charge Conference and the body with which the separately incorporated child care ministry relates on matters such as rent, use of shared space and staffing, ownership of furnishings and property, relationship with the pastor and church ministries, and expectations concerning church membership representation on their independent 501(c)3 board (including who gets to choose the representatives).

- Similarly, some churches have independently incorporated Local Church Foundations (*UM Discipline ¶2535*) instead of endowment committees. Since this arrangement creates a separately incorporated body, care will need to be taken to relate the governing board of the foundation to the congregation's leadership board and charge conference. This may require approving amendments to the bylaws of the foundation.

APPENDIX G

Report/Request for Action Form for Governing Board

Update/ Action Request for <u>(DATE)</u>_____

Please submit this form to the church office ten days prior to Leadership Board Meeting so it can be added to the agenda.

❑ **For Information Only** ❑ **Needs Action from Governing Board**

Committee or Ministry Team:
   ❑ Facilities Team ❑Worship Planning Team

   ❑ Ministry Team/Task Group:_____

   ❑ Staff:_____ (Staff should coordinate with pastor before submitting.)

Committee Chair/Team Leader Contact:

Name:

Email:

Phone:

ISSUE / PROPOSAL:

Use this section to explain the actions, key strategies, and/or challenges with which the committee or team is faced.
Include proposed solutions or strategic plans.

FINDINGS / RATIONALE:

Explain how the proposed action helps the congregation fulfill its mission and impact the mission field.

FUNDING IMPLICATIONS?

❑ **None beyond budgeted Annual Fund**

❑ **Yes. See below for costs and funding plan.**

*Financial Stewardship in a congregation requires advance
planning, teamwork, and discernment of priorities.
Fundraising beyond the Annual Fund can be delicate work.
Please include in this section the financial implications
of the proposal, and fundraising plans if Designated
Funds or additional support is required.*

ACTIONS TAKEN BY COMMITTEE / TEAM:

*Our congregation seeks to empower committees and
ministry teams to do ministry and take action, within
the guiding principles, strategic goals, and administrative
policies of the congregation. Use this section to outline
the actions planned or already taken by the
Committee/Team under its own authority.*

ACTIONS REQUIRING LEADERSHIP BOARD APPROVAL:

*This includes: Proposed changes in Policy or Guiding
Principles, actions requiring Fiduciary or Mandated Duties,
actions requiring changes in the Budget, and proposals
that would change a congregational strategic goal.*

APPENDIX H

Leadership Covenant Suggestions

In addition to the list below, you may wish to add other covenantal elements that define the roles and authority of each board member individually and collectively, such as boundaries about making demands upon staff and staff time without consulting the pastor, matters of conflicts of interest, and the limits of personal authority as an individual board member.

- Board members are encouraged to invest in conversations and decisions with vigor and passion. However, once the board has come to a decision, each board member will openly and publicly support the decision of the board whether the individual member personally agrees with the decision. We are a board with a unified voice.

- Board members are expected to be present at all board meetings unless ill or out of town. If members miss more than three meetings, the board chair will converse with the board member to see if their seat needs to be vacated and filled by someone who can be more active.

- Board members will review the meeting packet prior to meetings, coming fully prepared and ready to participate.

- Board members are role models for the congregation. Therefore, members will model mature discipleship by being present in worship at least three times per month, tithing or moving toward a tithe, have an active prayer life, serve in mission three times per year, be active in a ministry team, be in a faith development group, and openly share their faith with others in the secular world.

- Board members will be on time for meetings, silence cell phones, and immerse themselves in the meeting without distractions in respect for others' time and commitment.

- Board members will encourage and support our pastors and fellow board members.

- Board members will hold ourselves, the pastors, and other board members accountable for their leadership roles and responsibilities. This includes allowing others to hold the board members collectively and individually accountable.

- Board Members understand that conflict and disagreements are natural in any community, including the church. As a board, we will approach matters of disagreement with transparency and maintain our missional focus as a board. When approached by a person or group concerning a matter of disagreement or conflict, we will follow the path laid out by Jesus in Matthew 18 by encouraging the concerned party to go directly to the individual, to volunteer to go with the concerned party as a witness, or to invite the concerned party to address the full leadership or an assigned work team to address the issue. At no time will we support secret meetings that undermine the integrity or authority of the pastor or Board.

APPENDIX I

Guiding Principles

Potential Topics for Guiding Principle Consideration

- Mission, vision, core values of the church
- Identification the board's role, powers, responsibilities, and authority, in regards to the Book of Discipline
- Financial approval rules for staff, the pastor, and the building maintenance team
- Hiring/terminating authority of the pastor and other paid staff
- References to church wide policies:
    - Building and equipment usage policies (for example, rental policies for members, internal ministry groups, outside non-profit groups, or for-profit businesses)
    - Safe sanctuary policies for child protection
    - Employee handbook
    - Building safety
    - Internet usage
- Parliamentary rules of order, such as the usage of Robert's Rules of Order, the consensus method, or other variations
- Include how to change a guiding principle
- Official record keeping and access to records of meetings and executive session minutes
- Role and function of the building maintenance team
- Authority and responsibility of the treasurer
- Relationship of Nominations and Lay Leadership Development to the Leadership board
- Boundaries that state how individual board members may make (or not) demands on staff time outside formal board requests

- How daycare and/or preschool relate to the church, pastor, and leadership board (There is a huge legal and governance difference between childcare ministries that operate under a church's ministry and childcare ministries that exist as a separate but related 501(c)(3). These differences will impact how you write your guiding principle defining the relationship)

- Defining public meetings vs executive session (such as personnel matters when the board is operating as the congregation's S/PPRC).

Sample Guiding Principles

- All references to the Church Council, Board of Trustees, Staff/Pastor Parish Relations Committee, Endowment Committee, and Finance Committee, in all congregational policies as of _____, and in all references in the Book of Discipline of the United Methodist Church, shall be understood to refer to the Leadership Team beginning _____.

- Once the budget is approved, those responsible (i.e. staff and team leaders) for the various ministry areas have the authority to spend their budget to align with the objectives for their ministry area approved by the pastor. No further approval is needed to access the budget in their area of responsibility. *

- The pastor is responsible for reviewing line items within ministry areas with staff and team leaders for accountability from the staff and to the board.

- Any member of the Building Maintenance Team has the authority to purchase supplies for building maintenance and improvement up to $____ without approval. The Building Maintenance Team leader can authorize purchases for building maintenance and improvement up to $_____. Purchases up to $_____ can be approved by the pastor. Any purchases over $_____ need Leadership Board approval unless the expenditure is already approved in a capital expenditure line item in the approved budget. *

- Any expenditure over $_____ will require three bids. Preference will be given to hire local companies offering competitive bids within 5 percent of other bids. If the expenditure is already approved in the budget and meets the previous criteria, there is no further approval needed. *

- The pastor has the authority to hire and release employees using the church's employee policies. When terminating an employee, the pastor will invite a board member to sit in.

- The authority to hire and terminate employees of the church shall be vested in the Leadership Board. The pastor shall have the authority to interview and recommend candidates to fill open staff positions. The Board shall have the sole authority to determine the number of staff positions, approve job descriptions for each staff member, and set the salary paid to each staff member. The Leadership Board delegates to the pastor the authority to supervise, discipline, and manage paid staff.

- The pastor will review all paid staff annually using the approval evaluation process in the employee manual dated _____. Paid staff will review unpaid staff/team and leaders annually using the same evaluation process.

- The Weekday Child Care Advisory Board (*BOD* Paragraph 256.2.c) is fully amenable and accountable to the Leadership Board, and shall submit an annual budget and recommended policy changes to the Leadership Board. The director of weekday ministries is supervised by the pastor.

- The board recognizes and approves the Building Usage Policies dated _____.

- The board recognizes and approves the Building Security and Key Policies dated _____.

- The board recognizes and approves the Financial Controls Policies dated _____.

- All meetings of the Leadership Board shall be open to the public, with the exception of any meeting or portion of a meeting in which a personnel matter or a matter of legal negotiations is considered. In those cases, the Board will go into executive session. Minutes of executive session agenda items concerning personnel matters will be kept separately as part of the S/PPRC files.

- Leadership Board members are nominated by a separate and independent Nominating Committee, chaired by the pastor, and elected by the Charge Conference as described in the *BOD*. Due to Leadership Board's serving as the congregation's Staff-Parish Relations Committee, no immediate family member of the pastor or other paid staff person may serve as a member of the board. Due to serving as the congregation's Board of Trustees, only Leadership Board members over the age eighteen will have voting privileges in matters of property, incorporation, legal matters, contracts, insurance, investments, or other matters described in the *BOD* paragraphs 2525-2551.

---

* The treasurer must be consulted concerning any single purchase or expenditure over $_____ for purposes of cash flow. The treasurer does not approve or deny purchases but rather confirms large purchases will not create cash flow issues.

APPENDIX J

Monthly Board Agenda

AnyTown First United Methodist Church
Leadership Team Meeting
Date _____

Our Mission: To make new disciples of Jesus Christ for the transformation of the world.

Our Vision: Each of us at FUMC is on a journey to grow closer to God, to be more like Jesus, and to be filled with the Holy Spirit. No matter where you are in your walk with Christ, you are invited to journey and grow with us, through the power of the Holy Spirit, so that we can fulfill God's commission.

Core Values: Excellence, evangelism, engagement, equipping, expansion, and encouragement.

6:00pm	Opening Prayer	Jennifer Jackson, Chair
6:00pm	Spiritual Formation	David Dent
6:15pm	Leadership Equipping	Carol Clark
6:30pm	Review of New People	Pastor Taylor
6:35pm	Goal Review and Accountability Conversation	Pastor Taylor
6:50pm	Packet and Consent Calendar Items	
6:55pm	Generative and Strategic Work	Jennifer Jackson
	6:55: Item #1	
	7:05: Item #2	
	7:15: Item #3	
7:25	Communication	
7:30	Closing Prayer	Debbie Duncan

Next Meeting is (date)_____

Also from Kay & Blake

marketsquarebooks.com · amazon.com · cokesbury.com

IMPACT!
*Reclaiming the Call
of Lay Ministry*
Kay Kotan & Blake Bradford

Other Books

from Market Square

marketsquarebooks.com

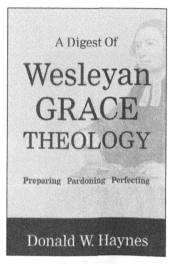

Wesleyan Grace
Theology

Dr. Donald Haynes

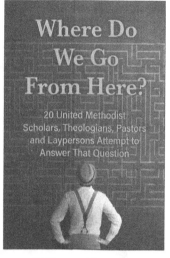

Where Do We
Go From Here?

20 United Methodist Writers

The Good Folks
of Lennox Valley

Kevin Slimp

The Methodist
Story

Dr. Donald Haynes

Grow Your Faith

with these books from Market Square

marketsquarebooks.com

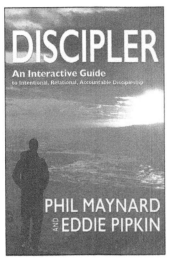

Discipler

Phil Maynard & Eddie Pipkin

Hear It, See It, Risk It

Steve Cordle

A Christian Teenager's Guide to Surviving High School

Ashley Conner

Understanding Your Call

11 Biblical Figures Understand Their Calls from God
by 10 United Methodist Leaders

Grow Your Faith

with these books from Market Square

marketsquarebooks.com

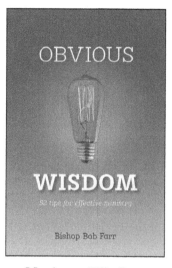

Obvious Wisdom

Bishop Bob Farr

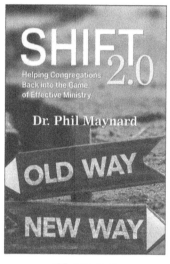

Shift 2.0

Phil Maynard

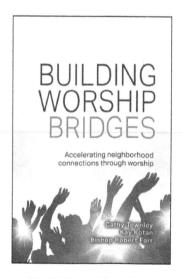

Building Worship Bridges

Cathy Townley

Get Out of that Box!

Anne Bosarge